Change of Heart

by
Bob White

ISBN-13: 978-1481167666

ISBN-10: 1481167669

For Loa

AKNOWLEDGEMENTS

The germ of thought that fired my muse to write this story began with an old man I saw walking out of the grocery store. He appeared to need help. When my wife, Loa, and I offered, he refused. After we watched him make it safely to his car, Loa said to me, "What if that was someone God sent to see if we cared?" I don't know the old gentleman's name, but I'm indebted to him.

No work of fiction, however, is created without the help of many others. I'm indebted to a writing group I've belonged to over the past few years who helped hone this story to its present form. Ann and "The Interrobangs" in Hemet.

I must also thank those "Beta Readers" who gave the penultimate draft a thorough critique. Carole, Holly, and Jennifer from the Internet Writing Workshop. Two trusted, local readers, Diane and Roni, also provided valuable input. My thanks and gratitude to all of you.

Any foibles and errors you might find are mine, and mine alone.

Chapter 1

On the bus trip home Elwin Hunter sensed someone following him. At a stop he went to the back seat so he could survey the riders. No strangers acted suspiciously. Most of them regular riders like himself. He chalked his feeling up to paranoia. The air conditioning on the bus couldn't keep up with the July heat. Sweat soaked his shirt and beaded on his brow. He was tired. His stop would come up at the next corner. He rang the buzzer.

Elwin took the first step down to get off the MTA bus at Slausen and Rimpau. Midway off, he smiled back up at the driver, "Take care, Miguel. See you tomorrow."

Miguel mumbled something unintelligible through a scowl. The door closed, with a pneumatic hiss and a clunk that nicked at Elwin's heel. The bus roared off, adding to the acrid smog that clogged the city. The July heat enveloped him. He wiped at the sweat dripping off his forehead with his shirtsleeve.

To Elwin, spreading a little cheer and hope to his co-workers, his neighbors, and even Miguel, seemed second nature. He'd always had a kind, gentle disposition, but sometimes the effort seemed so futile with these people. How long did he have to do this? How long did he have to blend in with those around him? How long must he study them? When would his real mission begin?

He needed a name when he came to the city and he thought Elwin sounded about right. He sighed as he stretched his slender frame trying to relieve the burning in the muscles of his back and arms. He could never quite get rid of the persistent ache left over from a day sorting through trash at the recycling center. Despite his discomfort, he whistled a light, airy tune as he trudged around the corner to his apartment four blocks away; a third floor efficiency unit with sporadic hot water. Ahhh! He smiled at the hopeful thought. Water, pouring down like rain to wash away the grit and grime. Not heaven, but as close as he could find here.

He yanked at the perpetually sticky entrance door to the apartment building; a dirty-yellow stucco cube. When it opened at last, he entered the narrow hallway. Two steps in he met Tiffany coming from her first floor unit. He suspected the name she used with her customers might be something else, but then again. . . It seemed so many people used names other than their real ones. Omnipresent facades to hide from others, or themselves. Elwin didn't know Tiffany's last name, fake or real, but knew by the clothes she wore; a too short skirt and low-cut blouse, she was going to work. She would find a john— or two, or three. A few quick tricks so she could score drugs and booze for herself and her lazy pimp boy-friend, Jahleel. No fresh black and blue marks marring the fair skin of her arms or face today. He smiled— a flash of gladness for her fortune. Maybe Jahleel, discovered beating on his bank didn't help business. The best customers wanted someone not covered with bruises. He wondered how he could ever reach the man. Would a life of depravity trap them both forever?

Elwin swiped at the ever-present sweat on his forehead. He tried to catch the girl's eye. "Hello Tiffany."

"Hi," she replied in a tiny voice, turning her head away.

"Be careful out there."

She stopped and focused on a broken tile in the floor, then back at Elwin. "Why do you always tell me to be careful, Mr. Hunter?"

Why did she always call him mister? "Because you should. Because it's sometimes a mean world." He paused a moment. "But you know that. . . and because you matter."

She flashed a quick smile and turned away.

He wondered, should he say it all? Because you matter to God. Maybe he should the next time. Maybe he could reach her. Without another word, he turned to continue his slow trek up the wooden steps. Like the rest of the building the stairwell smelled of dirt, and urine, and the occasional dead rodent.

"I'll be careful," she said to his back as she stepped out of the building.

At the second floor landing through a thin door he heard Mrs. Ramirez screaming threats and curses at her husband, then a crash and clatter as something fell to the floor. The yelling ceased abruptly, and a door inside the Ramirez' apartment slammed. When he tried to intervene once, a couple of months earlier, Jorge took a swing at him. He'd retreated to his apartment with a bloody nose. So much for altruism.

Elwin moved softly, trying not to make a sound, as he trudged up the bare stairs. He knew he shouldn't be afraid of Jorge, but he didn't want his nose bloodied again. At least his apartment was on the other side of the stairwell and one story higher, so he wouldn't have to listen to Carmen and Jorge below him banging around and screaming much of the night. It provided him enough distance, at least most of the time. Away from the noise. Away from the threat of another smack in the nose. One more flight for his tired legs to go and he'd be in the sanctuary of his apartment.

A low wattage naked bulb glowed on the third floor landing. Elwin made it a point to know who lived behind each of the other three doors, although no one knew him well, or each other for that matter. At least no one on this level had slugged him when he'd tried to talk with them during the previous six months. Times when he'd tried to spread a little cheer and peace.

Elwin fished in his pocket for a worn leather key-fob. He turned the bolt with a click and, by habit, pushed himself through the doorway, then stopped.

Something wasn't right. No light. He slid quickly into the darkness beside the door so he wouldn't silhouette himself in the light from behind. He could have sworn he'd pushed the drapes back and put the shades up before he left in the morning. Now down, they shut out almost all the light, the drapes pulled shut too. The possibilities flashed through his mind in milliseconds. Who'd been here? The building manager? He doubted it. Grouchy old Andy never came by, at least during the six months he'd lived there. Didn't even fix the leaky faucet or the plugged drain. No, not Andy the building manager. But certainly someone.

Even though Elwin didn't possess the keen abilities he'd once used he sensed a presence. He'd been right when he'd told Tiffany it can sometimes be a mean world. Could it be the enemy? Maybe his foreboding thoughts on the way home weren't far off the mark. No. Not possible. He'd been promised that wouldn't happen. Others were to watch out for him. Time to find out. "Who's there?"

"An old friend." The almost melodic, baritone voice overflowed with warmth. "Have a seat." An old lamp with a torn shade came to life across the room.

Elwin exhaled as he recognized the voice and the eyes. The rest of his visitor was different from the last time they'd been together. He hadn't realized how tense he'd grown. He took in a breath and let it out. Tried to relax. "It's good to see you, Sophio." He pulled a straight-backed wood chair away from the small breakfast table and collapsed on it. He took in Sophio's tailored pinstripe suit, crisp white shirt, and silk maroon tie. "I don't think I've seen you in human form before."

"It was thought best I blend in. Look like the rest of the people. Although for this place. . ." He shrugged. "Should I call you Elwin. . . or Paragon?"

"Elwin's probably best, at least in public. Won't arouse suspicions. I won't have to answer questions from my neighbors. You should have worn working people's clothes. Did anyone see you come or enter?"

"A frail elderly lady down the hall."

"Ahh. . . Mrs. Johnston. She's sweet, but has trouble remembering. I don't think she has much longer, but she's happy. Reads her Bible every day. Gives me little pamphlets with messages of God's love. I haven't told her anything about myself. She wouldn't understand, and there's no need."

Sophio chuckled. "She said something to me about her son. Apparently she mistook me for him. Told me he's coming to take her to his house, and she doesn't want to go."

"It was the suit. I don't blame her. I've met the son. He doesn't care about her. He's after her Social Security check."

A wry smile momentarily creased Sophio's face. "Maybe we can do something about that."

A silence hung in the air. Finally Elwin broke it. "So it looks like you snuck in almost undetected. I'm glad to see you. Truly I am. I wondered how long I'd be exiled here."

11

"It wasn't exile, Para—, excuse me. . . Elwin." He flashed a quick smile. "It was training."

"Yes. Yes." He paused. "So everyone told me."

"You have doubts?"

"No. Not really. I've never truly doubted. But it seems so. . . so unconnected."

"I understand."

Elwin frowned and shook his head. "I don't. How can this. . . this experience be training? Every day I've felt like an outcast."

"Just like the people in your apartment building must feel. But enough of that for now. We can revisit it later. You've done well in your six months here."

Elwin shook his head and frowned. "What are you saying? I don't think I've done anything at all."

"You've accomplished much." Sophio caught Elwin's gaze. "More importantly you've learned more than you realize, too."

"Like what, Sophio? For instance today at work Freddie grumbled about how his wife didn't pack him a decent lunch. Half a peanut butter sandwich. That's all. I know it's trivial, but. . ."

"But there's more?"

"Freddie, his wife, and their three kids live with her parents because they lost their house. It's not all their fault. Part of it's the economy. I felt sorry for him. He should have a little brightness. Something to let him know the whole world wasn't out to get him. I gave him an orange and a bag of chips. I told him, 'It's not a lot, but maybe it'll make your day lighter.'"

"And?"

"Well, you'd think he'd say thanks, or. . ." Elwin shook his head. "You'd think someone along the way would have taught. . . ." Sophio wouldn't understand. He let the thought die. "What did I accomplish by giving him something?"

"Maybe some day Freddie, will learn it is better to share, to give. . . and to be thankful, too."

Elwin shrugged. "Like that's going to happen."

"You're not turning pessimistic are you?"

Elwin hung his head. First, doubt. Now cynicism. So easy to lose touch with goodness. "I hope not. I try to guard against it."

"Though you can't see Freddie learning much about giving or being thankful, you should know you've given a bit of a lift to Tiffany. She might lead a troubled life, but she's still open. And, believe it or not, she's seeking a way out of her quagmire. It shouldn't be too much longer 'til she makes a leap to safety."

"Ahhh. You have me at a disadvantage. I'm not at liberty to follow her around. . . unseen."

Sophio flashed the slightest hint of a smile. "True, but your words of concern have stayed with her. You've given her confidence for the present."

"I hope so. I worry how she's treated."

"She'll be fine. You've lived so long without any contact from us it's easy to forget it's not the body, but the spirit and the soul that matter."

Elwin nodded. "You're right. Living here, like I have, it's easy to allow the mundane to crowd out that knowledge." He took in a breath and let it out. "So what happens with me and these people now?"

"You'll find out in good time. Even Jorge Ramirez' fist against your nose will probably serve you well."

Elwin leaned forward. "You know about that?"

"Oh yes." He chuckled. "When you took this assignment your eyes were blinded to the supernatural. It's why you haven't seen any of us, but we've been here." Sophio paused a beat, leaned forward. "Constantly. In the process your thinking, the way you feel, has undergone a change. It's time for the next step."

"The next step?"

"Of course." Sophio smiled and began to glow with an ethereal aura. "The time you've spent wasn't an end to itself, merely the beginning. The training—"

"What's going to happen?"

"First, you must return with me. Michael has requested your presence. Then, perhaps later, I can tell you a story."

Why did Michael want to see him? "When do we go? What story?"

"We must go now. My story will come in due time."

Worry lines creased Elwin's face. "But, I should shower. I need to clean up. I don't want to go before Michael looking like this."

"You forget. You can be changed. As Paul wrote to the church at Corinth two millennia ago, 'in the twinkling of an eye.' So, my friend, shall we go?"

Elwin closed his eyes and nodded. "I think I've forgotten how."

Sophio glowed with a brilliant light as he reached out and grasped Elwin's arm.

In an instant they both vanished from the apartment.

Chapter 2

Two old men slouched in a dark corner of the alley across the street from Elwin's apartment building. The shorter one said, "Did you see the flash in the window, Master? They must have called him back."

"Of course." The larger one scowled as he spit out the words. "But he'll return. I know them. The enemy won't quit that easily. You must be vigilant. You must use all your powers to keep their plan from succeeding, my dear Alderon."

"I will, Master." Alderon knelt and kissed the back of the hand held before him. "I'll not fail. Not this time." A shiver racked his frame. "Not like my brother, Wormwood did in England during the war."

"Watch Paragon when he comes back. Take note of who he visits. It'll be someone he's known or befriended. You're familiar with the weaknesses each one of them has." He lowered his voice and bent close to Alderon. "Work on turning their weakness into a fatal flaw." He gripped Alderon's shoulder momentarily. "Pay attention too, to the form Paragon takes. Counter him at every turn. You don't want to fail and be scorned by all the host in our army." The master's eyes glowed with burning intensity. "You don't want to end up like your brother. . . in the pits. You must succeed."

Alderon bent his head, unable to hold back a smile of satisfaction. He'd been entrusted with a noble task. "Yes, Heylel." When Alderon raised his eyes he saw only a brick wall.

Chapter 3

Paragon found Sophio sitting on an expanse of grass under a Jacaranda tree. Its pale lavender blooms blanketed the ground around him. Some of the blossoms rested on his flaxen hair. They fluttered to the ground, a kaleidoscope of violet petals, as his friend stood. He heard the faint sound of a thousand voices drifting on the ether, from a distance, as they sang an anthem of adoration.

Sophio embraced him with a hearty hug. His blue eyes held Paragon's gaze as they broke apart. "Well? What did Michael say?"

"There's not much to tell. He did say though, someone would be sent to me when I needed help. I asked what kind of help and . . . well, you know Michael. He gave me a broad smile, and said I'd have to trust Him."

"So, I gather your mission is a secret one."

"Perhaps not so much secret as liberating for those I must meet."

"Do you know who they are?"

"Oh yes. Altogether, seven. I've lived near most of them for the past six months. Some are people in the apartment building where I stayed." He ticked them off on his fingers. "Then there's my co-worker Freddie, Mrs. Johnston's son, and Miguel who drives the bus. They all should be here with us someday, even Jorge and Tiffany. They should be with our Lord. The way they think now, they don't believe it's possible. They think they need to earn it when Michael has paid the price and given it to them. They need a new mind-set. Michael called it a change of heart. One way to do that is to give them a little jolt of reality."

"Ahh. . . I know exactly what you're talking about. If they only knew. . ." Sophio shook his head in wonder. "If they realized Michael doesn't want anyone missing. But they are sometimes so stubborn and thick-headed."

Paragon nodded. "They are that."

Sophio sat back down. "You have a difficult task. When do you return?"

"I have to leave soon." The smile faded from Paragon's face. "I must go alone, Sophio, and I can't return to them as Elwin." He closed his eyes and sighed.

"Did Michael tell you why?"

"I must visit them as a stranger. Someone they don't know or recognize."

Worry lines crunched between Sophio's eyes. "So your past friendship won't help?"

"True." Paragon looked with a steady gaze at his friend. "But I'll again have the advantage of using the powers Michael has given us."

Sophio patted the ground beside him. "Here. Can you talk with me a minute?"

Paragon sat cross legged on the grass, among the lavender blossoms, facing his companion.

"You have a difficult mission. Can I be so bold as to ask how you will accomplish your task?"

"When the time is ripe I will be a victim for them

to experience the joy of loving and caring. They need to experience Michael's love flowing through them. I'm excited about my task." Paragon's voice fell to a whisper, "But afraid too."

Sophio gripped Paragon's arm. "A victim?"

"Michael said you would know and understand."

A faraway look settled in Sophio's eyes. "Ahh, yes. Now I understand why one of us might need to come to your aid. And I think it's time to tell you my story."

"Go on."

"When Michael went to live among them to make his sacrifice. I believe, at the time, you'd been assigned to be the guardian for Liu Hsiu. You needed to keep him from danger, so he could effect reforms for his people.

Paragon nodded.

"Michael told a story about a man set on by thieves. Two religious leaders saw him at the side of the road, and refused to help. Finally an outcast from Samaria rescued him."

"I heard the tale. Read it too when I assumed the form of Elwin."

"It's not a fable, or a story, Paragon."

Paragon leaned forward. "What? I thought—"

"The attack and rescue really happened." Sophio gazed off into the clouds for a moment. "Not many know, but I was the one beaten by thieves."

"You?"

"Yes, so Michael could answer a lawyer's question about the way to life."

"Did he learn?"

Sophio pursed his mouth and shook his head. "I'm afraid not. . ." then his visage brightened. "But others did."

"So," Paragon said, "when I'm a victim— if everyone walks by?" He hoped for reassurance.

Something more than a smile.

Sophio grasped his arm and gave it a squeeze. "Someone will help. If it's not Jorge or one of the others, you won't be left. I'm sure one of us will be sent to your aid.

"Perhaps it will be you, my friend."

"Perhaps. We'll see." He took a breath. "Now, tell me do you know who you will work with first?"

"My old co-worker, Freddie. Michael said even now the enemy is plotting against my work."

"That's to be expected. What's planned for Freddie?"

"Remember old Job a few millennia ago?"

"Of course. How could any of us forget?"

"Well, Freddie is about to experience a loss or two of his own. Not as severe as Job, but damage just the same. His home's been foreclosed. His wife has lost her job. He's having a difficult time dealing with the stress of living with his in-laws." Paragon paused. "However, that might be the one good thing working for him."

"So what happens?"

"I'll start by giving him a helping hand, then we'll see if he can give me one when he's really down."

A seraph approached the pair and whispered in Paragon's ear.

"It's time, Sophio. I must go."

"Take care Paragon. May peace and love go with you."

Chapter 4

Freddie Poyner slammed his hand against the steering wheel and spit out a curse. Six red lights in a row. Stuck in crawling traffic. Already late for work at the recycling yard. He knew his boss, lard bucket Alfred, would ream him a new one as soon as he walked through the gate. "You'd think I could get a break," he muttered aloud as he often did while driving. His thoughts drifted. Nothing had gone right since they lost the house. "What else can happen?"

No one answered.

A nano-second after the light turned green he laid on the horn. "Come on you idiot. Move it. Can't you see?" His fingers drummed a staccato beat on the wheel. As the car in front inched forward he said, "About time, jerk."

Freddie resumed his slow pace north through the morning traffic on Vernon, finally turning west on Jefferson. He wished he still had his cell phone so he could let Alfred know he was on his way to feed him some excuse. But they'd given the phones up, along with the house, after Georgia lost her job.

Six blocks from work Freddie's fifteen year old

Subaru gave a final chug and stopped. To the cacophony of irate motorists behind him he cranked the engine over repeatedly until the battery gave out. Somehow he'd have to shove the car over to the side of the road. A dumb piece of junk. That's what it was.

He turned his head to a knocking at the passenger side window. A homeless person in jeans and a dingy shirt had leaned his cardboard sign against a nearby light post and was motioning Freddie to roll down the window. He opened it an inch.

"You steer. I'll give you a push around the corner." The guy looked skinny and frail, not to mention that he needed a shave. Probably a bath, too. Well, whatever. Some help was better than none. It would stop the ruckus of blaring horns and shouted epithets behind him.

Freddie said, "You sure?" His question floated into the open air.

The man already stood behind the ancient Subaru. Freddie shifted into neutral as the homeless guy leaned against the trunk and the car began to roll. Freddie turned right onto a cross street, checked for no parking signs, and aimed for a vacant spot against the curb.

He called back to the man as he got out. "Thanks."

The man stopped, turned briefly and smiled through his week's growth of beard. "No problem. Everyone needs a little help from time to time. I didn't do much. Maybe it'll brighten your day later on."

What was that about? Freddie picked his lunch sack off the seat, locked the car, and began to trudge toward Jefferson. Alfred would be fuming now. When he reached the corner, a mere fifty feet from the car, he turned to look for the homeless man. The sign still leaned against the light post, but the homeless dude was nowhere to be seen. Strange. Weird, that's what it was.

His mother-in-law would have said it was an angel

and to give a little prayer of thanks. Yeah, right. Why did women always think like that? Freddie trudged down the street. Hey, you worked hard. You did your best, and sometimes it didn't pan out too good. You just went on; although going on now was beginning to wear on him. The seven of them crammed into three bedrooms at his in-laws' house. In a way he guessed they were lucky. They could be without any place to stay like the derelict who had pushed his car.

When he was a block away from the recycling yard what the street person said to him rang a bell. That was the kind of stuff Elwin would spout. But Elwin was gone. Up and quit without giving notice a week ago. Now, he'd met two crazy people in the world, and it was time to face old lard bucket.

To Freddie's amazement Alfred didn't say a word about being late when he clocked in. Alfred even sent him to pick up a load of copper wire across town in the company truck because their driver was sick. On his lunch break Freddie used a pay phone to call home. He needed to have Georgia or his father in law, Mason, pick him up after work. He told Georgia about the car giving up the ghost, and they'd have to find a way to repair it. Without the car he'd have to find a new way to work the next morning.

When Freddie clocked out at the end of the day Alfred waddled up beside him and smiled. Alfred never smiled. "Before you go, Poyner, I need to see you in my office for a minute."

He fantasized. Maybe he was being promoted to permanent driver. Freddie followed Alfred's ambling bulk into the windowless unpainted office.

His boss collapsed into a groaning chair behind a beat up desk, took out a soiled handkerchief, and wiped at the beads of perspiration on his swarthy face. "Have a seat, Poyner."

Freddie sat. Finally, something good was going to happen. The crazy bum had said something about his day being brighter, although he didn't believe it at the time.

"I got a problem here, Poyner."

"What problem, sir?"

"How late were you coming in today?"

This wasn't going to be a promotion. Maybe his pay docked again. "About half an hour. You see, my car broke down on the way. I had to walk."

"That's not my problem."

Freddie wanted to say something.

Alfred continued without a pause. "I'll tell you what my problem is, Poyner. You coming in late. Six times this month. That's my problem. I have an easy way to solve it. You're not going to be late any more, Poyner."

"No sir, I—"

Alfred yanked the top desk drawer open and pulled out a pink envelope. "This is your pay through today and a week's severance." He tossed the envelope across the desk. "Now, get out of my office. I don't ever want to see your ugly, whining face again."

Fired. Freddie stood in shock. He scooped up the pay envelope in a trembling hand and stumbled into the smog laden air. Some bright day it turned out to be. How would they feed the kids? Where could he find work with people losing jobs all across the country? It didn't matter much now if they fixed the old Subaru tonight.

Chapter 5

Two scruffy men loitered outside the gate of the recycling center. The older one spat on the ground.

Heylel said, "Look at him, Alderon. See his shuffling gait as he leaves work. This is your opportunity. He's discouraged. He needs to dwell on how bad life has treated him. Encourage his selfish thoughts any way you can."

"I will, Master."

"You were ingenious in getting his car to quit this morning. It almost seemed too easy. A shame Paragon stepped in as a bum to help. You should have found a way to stop him. We must outsmart the enemy. If Paragon gains too much influence in Freddie's life. . ." a sharp scowl twisted Heylel's face. "Need I say what the result might be?"

"I'll do my best to keep Paragon busy with other good deeds. Minimize his influence on Freddie."

"That's the way. Outmaneuver the enemy. And hound this subject. Don't let him get away from you. Use whatever you can, any temptation. Remember he's especially susceptible to pride and selfishness."

"Except for his wife he's easy prey at home. He

25

rankles at the compassion there. His in-laws seem to drive him toward us." A grin split Alderon's face. "It shouldn't be too many days and he'll be so solidly in our camp with his poor-me attitude. He'll never leave."

"Selfishness will win again, my dear Alderon. Selfishness must win. Keep up the good work."

Alderon watched Freddie shuffle toward the bus stop. When he turned back Heylel couldn't be seen.

Chapter 6

Freddie sat at the breakfast table and sighed as he stared at a half empty mug. He hated cold coffee. It didn't taste good. It didn't even smell good. At the sound of a footfall he lifted his head to see Georgia coming into the kitchen. Forty-one and, to Freddie, she was still as beautiful as the day they'd married, despite the dark circles under her eyes. Even though lines etched her face, Georgia was the bright spot in his life. But now he worried about her. "You look tired, honey," he said. "Take a break. Let me get you a cup of coffee."

Georgia sat at the table beside Freddie and patted his hand. "I'll be fine. The kids are off to school. I'll rest after you go."

Freddie brought her a cup of coffee anyway. "I'll find a job pretty soon. You shouldn't worry so much."

She tucked a stray strand of dark chestnut hair behind her ear. "I'm not worried, Freddie. We'll survive this. Last night my dad told me that he doesn't want us to pay our share of the food and utilities until you get a job."

"I don't want no charity, Georgia. Your folks mean well, but a man's got his pride. First, your dad paid to get our car back from the shop, now the groceries. I feel like a bum. I lost the house. I can't support my family." He hammered his clenched hand on the table. The coffee splashed from the cups into little puddles.

She put her hand atop his and gave it a quick squeeze. "It's not your fault Freddie. The economy's in the dumps and we're down on our luck right now. Things are hard for lots of people." She paused a moment. "I. . . I could try to find a job, too. Maybe waitress or something."

"No." He pulled his hand back. "I won't have you supporting me. Not like that. Strangers flirting with you. No, Georgia." Freddie said it with too much force and immediately regretted it. He dropped his head and stared at the coffee mug.

"Okay. Okay. We can wait till later, when you've got a good job again, and we get our own place. Don't fret. I won't waitress."

Deflated now. "I'm sorry, Georgia. It's just. . ." His thought died.

She covered his clenched fist with her small soft hand. "It's all right. I understand. Things'll get better. I know they will. Sometimes you just have to believe." She gave his hand another gentle squeeze.

Freddie took a deep breath, relaxed his fist and tried to smile. "That's my Georgia. The eternal optimist. I don't know what I'd do. . . You're. . ." He let the words trail off.

She colored slightly. "Oh, Freddie."

He fell silent for a moment. "If I still had my job we'd be okay. I'd feel better. It's bad enough us having to stay with your folks and them paying for stuff."

"Now, now, Freddie, don't fuss about it."

"Maybe today I'll find something." He looked at the clock. "I better get going."

"You have your list?"

He patted his shirt pocket. "Right here. Twelve places today from last night's paper."

She stood as he rose to go and grabbed his hand, then pulled him toward her, not letting him leave. "A hug and a kiss from my man before you go on the road." When they broke apart she said, "I'll say a prayer for you while you're out there."

Freddie said, "A lot a—"

"Shush, now. It does too work. You just have to be in tune. Now off with you." She kissed him again on the cheek.

The sun cooked the city. Not even a breeze stirred the smoggy air as Freddie walked out of the tenth business on his list. The places he'd gone to fill out an application for work all gave him different versions of the same story. No openings. Two let him fill out an application, but didn't give him any hope of being hired.

A bag lady shuffling down the sidewalk accosted him. "Hey mister. . ." Her voice cracked and she blinked at him with rheumy eyes. "Can you spare some change?"

He looked her over. Grime in the creases of her skin. Dirty clothes; rags really. From four feet away he could smell her. Freddie didn't want to get close enough to give her anything let alone touch her.

"Please." She stretched out a soiled hand with cracked and jagged fingernails. "I'm hungry. I could use a meal."

He had ten bucks in his pocket, but that was for gas to get home and to go hunting for work again tomorrow. Ten dollars he knew came from Georgia's father. He spit out the words, "I don't got nothing." He turned his head away and stepped to the far edge of the sidewalk as he hurried away. Go get a job. Earn your own money. Buy your own food, or rot-gut wine. Get lost.

She followed him down the street like an abandoned puppy with an empty belly. "Please mister," she whined. "You got a quarter or somethin'?"

Freddie picked up the pace, almost running to his waiting Subaru, climbed inside, and slammed the door. The car cooked him like an oven, but he felt safe inside his metal cocoon as he sped away leaving the beggar-woman in his exhaust fumes.

He still had two more places on his list. Maybe he could wrangle an interview if they had an opening. He wanted to have good news for Georgia when he finished for the day.

That night after the kids were in bed Georgia herded him to their bedroom and away from her mother's solicitous questions.

He smelled a hint of his favorite perfume. What a woman. Even here at his in-laws she did everything she could to make him feel good. Tonight he needed that.

"Tomorrow's another day," she said as the door closed. "You'll find something soon."

"I been at it for over two weeks, Honey." He sat on the edge of the bed, hung his head and stared at a spot on the floor. "Eighty-nine places, Georgia. Eighty-nine. I'm running out of prospects. It tears me up inside taking charity from your folks. I don't know how much longer I can take it."

"You're a good man. It doesn't matter how long it takes," she said sitting close beside him. "I love you. The kids love you."

"Love ain't enough, Georgia. I gotta—"

She held his hand, entwined her fingers with his. "How do you know? Maybe it is. You just need to believe. . . even when it seems impossible."

"I don't know."

She put her arm across his shoulders and pulled him close. "Love's enough for me. It's enough for Ricky and Toni and little Ed. We'll get by. Things'll get better."

He shook himself away. "Naw. Not for me. Your folks are rubbing off on you. Be happy, and if things go wrong, pray about it. Not for me, Georgia. You know I don't believe in that stuff."

She fell silent for a moment, then put her arm around Freddie's shoulder again. "I'm sorry you don't." She said no more. A tear leaked out, and she turned her head away.

Freddie couldn't stand the silence between them. "I gotta go. Gotta get gas in the car for tomorrow."

"What?"

"I forgot on my way home." He pulled himself away from Georgia and stalked out the door.

Chapter 7

Freddie Poyner remembered them all as he drove home from his first night on the job. One hundred ninety seven. That's how many applications he'd filled out, that and twenty three interviews across the city, before Best Maintenance hired him. Emptying wastebaskets, cleaning smelly toilets, and mopping floors wasn't much of a job, but it promised a paycheck at the end of the week. Most important, though, he could pay his own way now. That would keep Georgia's parents off his back. The thought brought a smile to his lips, and he began to whistle a tune. A melody he remembered from when he courted Georgia. First time in weeks he'd felt in high spirits.

He knew in his heart and soul the reason he'd been hired was because he kept plugging away, day after day, one job application after another. To Freddie's way of thinking there wasn't any free lunch. You had to do everything on your own. Georgia said they'd hired him because she prayed about it every day. Freddie knew better. The idea of getting help from God. . . Nothing more than a pipe-dream. Anyone who had any sense of the real world knew that whole religious hocus pocus stuff was for weaklings. His Georgia was kind and sweet and he wondered sometimes why she believed so much religious hogwash. Probably because of her parents. Soon he'd be able to take her away from that. As soon as they promoted him to foreman or lead. His fingers played on the steering wheel in time to his music. Not even the stop and go morning traffic on the four lane boulevard bothered him.

The accident happened so fast Freddie hardly had time to react. The car in front of him obviously didn't see the homeless woman in gray rags pushing the grocery cart loaded with her possessions. That, or they didn't care. The driver didn't swerve or even hit the brakes. He mowed down the cart and kept on driving so he could sneak through the yellow light ahead.

Freddie pulled to a stop, turned on the old Subaru's emergency flashers, and jumped out to survey the damage. The mangled grocery cart lay on its side, plastic bags and clothing lay strewn in the gutter along with a cardboard sign. It said, HUNGRY - PLEASE HELP - GOD BLESS YOU. The woman had fallen to the pavement. One of her arms was bent at an odd angle. He saw blood, but not a lot. Still, she needed help.

By this time the driver from the car behind Freddie had joined him and was talking on his cell phone. "Yes," he said. "Hit and run. Two cars in front of me. The lady needs an ambulance."

Freddie did a double take at the guy on the phone who wore baggy jeans and a bright yellow sweat-shirt proclaiming he loved Jesus in bright blue, gothic letters, then turned his attention to the woman. When he knelt down he recognized her. The lined skin, the pinched face, the ragged clothes, the rheumy eyes looking up at him. This time, for some reason, it didn't matter that she smelled like she hadn't bathed in weeks. "Help's coming," he said. He nodded his head toward the other motorist. "That guy's calling nine-one-one. You need to lie still 'til the ambulance comes. Okay?"

She nodded. Tried to smile. "God bless you for stopping."

A fortnight's guilt welled up. "I'm sorry."

"You didn't hit me."

"I know. I'm sorry about not giving you money for food."

The woman looked at him with expressionless eyes.

"You don't remember?"

"Oh, I do. But I forgave you." Her breath came in wheezing gasps. "You must learn to forgive yourself. You'll feel better."

Freddie didn't know what to say. A strange feeling washed over him immersing him in warmth and energy. "Does your arm hurt bad?" he managed to ask.

She grimaced as she tried to move it. "Not too bad." Her voice was just a hoarse whisper.

Freddie could hear the wail of a siren in the distance. Cars from the opposing traffic streamed down the street, but no one stopped. "Help's almost here." Freddie turned to talk to the guy in the yellow sweatshirt who'd called, but he was gone. His car gone, too. Probably drove away. The traffic that Freddie thought would back up behind him had pulled into the other lane and flowed by. How weird, he thought, as he stared down the street searching for the flashing red lights of the ambulance. It was just him and the old woman waiting for help while the traffic whizzed along. When he turned to make sure she was okay, she was gone too. The grocery cart lay on its side against the curb, the bags and loose clothes still strewn in the gutter. A dream? No. He knew he couldn't be dreaming about the whole thing.

The sign had been folded into a tent and perched on the sidewalk. The bottom line was all that showed. GOD BLESS YOU.

The ambulance pulled to a stop behind Freddie's car and the siren died. A female EMT hopped out of the passenger side and strode toward him. "You should sit down, sir. Where are you hurt?"

"I'm not hurt. There was an old homeless lady hit by a car that drove off. That's her shopping cart and stuff. She was here just a minute ago. I think she had a broken arm."

"A broken arm? Where did she go?"

"I don't know. I turned away for a minute to see the guy who called. I saw your lights flashing, and when I looked back she was gone. The guy that called on his cell phone is gone too."

"Are you sure you're feeling all right?" The medical technician put her hand on Freddie's forehead. "Look at me. Let me see your eyes."

What would it take for her to believe him?

It took forty minutes with the EMT and the cops who came to investigate the accident, but finally they told him he could go home. He picked up the cardboard sign, and put it on the front passenger seat.

As he pulled into the driveway at his in-laws he was still debating whether to tell Georgia about his experience. Maybe he should. He knew she'd believe him. He grabbed the sign off the seat and went inside.

Georgia was cleaning up the kitchen. Their kids were off to school and her parents had left for work. Peace and quiet. No prying questions. She turned and smiled at him as he closed the door. "How was your first day? I guess I should say night."

"Okay, I guess. At least it means a paycheck."

"What's with the cardboard?"

"Oh this," he said, placing the still folded sign gently on the kitchen counter. "You better sit down."

"You didn't take that from someone did you?"

"Gosh, no."

"Well?"

"It was the weirdest thing, Georgia. Happened on my way home. There were times when I thought I was dreaming. The cops and the ambulance lady thought I was nuts or drunk."

"You weren't in an accident?"

"No, honey. I'm fine. Now listen. I brought the cardboard just to prove to myself that it wasn't a dream, that I didn't imagine it."

When Freddie finished his tale Georgia said, "You know what I think?"

"Yeah. I know what you think. You think it had something to do with angels or stuff like that. I almost didn't bring that stupid sign home and tell you because I knew what you'd think." Freddie stopped and sighed. "But the whole thing was so strange. Just plain bizarre. And when the homeless woman talked to me I felt this sense of. . . I don't know. . . like electricity going through me and. . . and peace."

"Maybe that was because you did something for someone else."

Freddie grunted.

"And back to what I think. If it wasn't an angel, Freddie, who was it?"

Freddie shook his head. Was she right? "I'm beat, Georgia. I'm going to bed. Wake me up when the kids come home from school, okay?"

"Sure." Georgia picked up the sign from the table, patted it gently, and held it close to her heart while she looked at her husband. "You gave a little of yourself today. God did bless you, Freddie."

A little of the same warmth he felt when he helped the homeless woman flooded through Freddie as he trudged to their bedroom, questions roaring though his mind in a perfect storm.

Chapter 8

At seven-sixteen in the evening the city began to slow down from the day's hustle of work and shopping. Even so, people still milled about on the city sidewalks. Freddie surmised they were going out to eat or the movies. Only the night workers, like him, were headed to toil. Freddie Poyner felt good. At least as good as he could feel since his mind kept flashing back to the accident he'd witnessed a few days before. He now called it the incident. He tried to shove it into a dark corner of his mind, but it never stayed there for long.

That morning his supervisor handed him his first paycheck, and he'd tucked it in his wallet before going home. After he'd slept, Georgia sent him off early to cash it just before their credit union closed, then speed across the city to his job. He still had over forty minutes before he needed to clock in. Tomorrow, he thought, he and Georgia would pay their share of the rent, buy some groceries, and maybe a treat for the kids. The beginning of independence from his in-laws beckoned. He whistled a happy tune and drummed on the steering wheel with his fingers, trying to quell the troubling thoughts about what happened when he tried to help the homeless woman. How could she get up from the gutter and leave with a broken arm?

Impossible, he thought. It couldn't be, but there she was. The glare of a street light shone down on her as she pushed her cart along the sidewalk. A freeway overpass with its shelter from the weather appeared to be her destination. When the signal turned green he couldn't help himself. He needed answers and it didn't matter how she looked. . . or smelled. Freddie drove his gasping Subaru around the corner and pulled to the curb.

"Pardon me, ma'am," he shouted as he jumped from the car and raced across the street.

The woman stopped and looked up when he neared. A smile cracked her face. Her ice blue eyes shone clear today. "How are you?" she said, still smiling.

"You're the lady the car hit the other day, aren't you?"

She nodded.

"I should ask how you are."

"I'm okay." She turned and grabbed hold of her cart to continue on her way.

"Don't leave. I thought you'd broken your arm. When the ambulance came, no one believed me."

"My arm's fine. I'm sorry they didn't believe you. That sort of thing happens all the time with God's children."

"But I—" Freddie stopped in mid sentence. Confusing thoughts flashed through his mind in rapid sequence. Did she mean I'm God's child? Naw. That couldn't be. How did people know that? But I didn't believe Georgia about the angels. . . What does it mean? It's all so weird. Why did I feel this. . . this unexplainable feeling? He couldn't help himself. "Here." Freddie reached for his wallet and pulled out a handful of bills and thrust them at the beggar woman. "Take this."

She shook her head.

"I know. . . I'm trying to make up. . ."

"No. I'm fine."

"Please. I know you can use it." He grabbed her hand and placed the money in her palm. When he touched her, the same jolt of warmth and energy he'd felt when he tended her at the accident coursed through his body.

"God bless you," she said.

"How do you do that?"

"Oh it's easy. . . and it wasn't me. It was you." She let the words settle on him. "You became a channel for love to flow through. I think you'll grow to enjoy it. Just keep doing what you did."

Freddie stared at her, as a sensation of energy and joy filled him.

"Oh, don't worry, your money will not be wasted." She smiled and shuffled away, hunched over her grocery cart.

Freddie put the wallet in his back pocket and crossed the street to his car. He couldn't believe this either. What was happening to him? What could he tell Georgia when he went home after a night's work? How would they buy groceries? They'd be stuck at his in-laws longer.

෯ ෯ ෯ ෯

Over the past week and a half he'd grown to expect the usual morning scene. Georgia tidying up in the kitchen, their kids off to school, and her parents at work. She turned and smiled at him as he closed the door.

"You look down, honey," she said as she gave him a peck on the cheek. "What's the matter?"

Freddie hung his head. "I did somethin' stupid, Georgia."

"There's nothing love can't cover," she said.

39

"This is pretty bad."

"You want to tell me now, or when you get up before the kids come home? You know I love you no matter what you did."

"This is really dumb. I won't be able to sleep. I gotta tell you."

"Let's sit. You want a glass of milk?"

"No, nothing." Freddie sat, pulled out his wallet, and laid it on the kitchen table.

Georgia sat opposite him and reached across to hold his rough hand in her soft, small one. "So, tell me, honey. What happened?"

"Remember when I brought home the sign the bag lady left after her accident?"

"Uh-huh."

"On my way to work last night I saw her."

"She's all right then?"

"Yeah. She's all right. I stopped to talk to her, Georgia. I don't know why, guilt maybe."

"You shouldn't feel bad. You did everything you could."

"But, Georgia, the accident was the second time I saw her."

Georgia's eyes widened. "What?"

"The first time was when I was out hunting for work." He ducked his head so he wouldn't have to look at her. "She begged for money and I told her to get lost. So last night. . ."

"You felt sorry for her? Wanted to help her? You felt guilty?"

Freddie nodded.

"You gave her some money from your first paycheck?"

His throat constricted. His stomach felt like it flipped over. "Yeah."

"That's not dumb. I'm proud of you." She patted his hand. "You did the right thing."

"No, Georgia. I said I did something stupid. I gave her almost all the money." Freddie pushed his wallet across the table. "Here. Look."

Georgia opened the wallet. She looked in it, then at Freddie. "I think it's all here Freddie." She pulled out a stack of bills and counted. "How much did you have?"

"Three hundred and thirteen dollars," Freddie mumbled as he stared wide-eyed at the money. "I don't understand. Where did that money come from?"

"I think I know, and even if you deny it, you do too."

Freddie shook his head. He'd heard stories like that as a little kid when his parents sent him to Sunday School, fish and bread multiplying, flour and oil never running out. Even then they all seemed so impossible. What he couldn't deny was the surge of energy and euphoria that coursed through him when he tended the woman, and when he gave her the money.

Georgia stood. "You go to bed, honey. I'm going to walk to the little church down the street and give God a thank offering."

"Would you mind if I went with you? Your angel, or whoever she was, said giving made me feel good."

Georgia smiled and took his hand. "I'd like that."

Chapter 9

Alderon used his powers to remain unseen as he followed Freddie and Georgia down the street to the church. He passed through the old oak doors and huddled in a corner. He couldn't stand to look at the cross in the front of the small chapel. He averted his eyes from the stained glass windows with their symbols of cross, crown, and dove. Being this close to images of the enemy sent a shiver up his spine.

Freddie and Georgia walked up the center aisle hand in hand. When they reached the front they sat on a pew.

Alderon sidled along the wall until he was within earshot of the couple who now spoke in whispered tones.

Freddie turned to Georgia. "What do we do now?"

"I'm not sure. I looked for a collection box of some sort, but I didn't see anything. Maybe we should just say a prayer and leave the offering on the table at the front."

"I don't know. I'd feel funny praying in public."

"This isn't public, Freddie. There's no one else here."

A side door near the front of the sanctuary opened. A gray-haired man in a black suit walked toward them. He smiled as he approached. "How can I help you? Do you have a question?"

"We came to give a thank offering, but didn't see any place to leave it."

"There's a small wood box near the entrance doors. Perhaps you missed it. You can stay here to meditate or pray as long as you like, and give your offering when you leave." The man smiled. "And God bless you." He turned and went back through the door leaving the two of them alone.

Freddie rose. "Let's go put our offering in the box. I wonder why we didn't see it when we came in?"

Alderon watched them walk out of the church and leave an offering in the box. He shivered again. This time not at the symbols of the enemy, but at the thought of what Heylel would say to him when they next met.

Chapter 10

Tiffany Clarke edged through the doorway and slid against the cold wall of the Wayfarer's Mission. She saw no one. The place smelled faintly of pine cleaner and lemon polish. Should she go farther in? She took a step, then hesitated. Her back pressed hard against the wall. It was a little past nine o'clock on a Thursday night. Hunger gnawed at her stomach, but hunger was the least of her worries. The chills had begun an hour earlier. The hunger she could live with. The chills, she knew, were because she needed a fix. And she needed it bad. But she'd made up her mind. Tonight she'd do it.

She craved freedom from her demon-infested prison. She needed to escape from her living hell. . . or die from an overdose, and she didn't want to die. Huddled against the wall, she remembered the horror of going through withdrawal before, and not of her own choosing. The panic, the nausea, the muscle cramps during those first two or three days created its own special kind of Hades. A hell worse than the dirty cell she'd been dumped in back then. The memory of that burning torment kept her imprisoned until she walked through the Mission's dingy door. A chill, more like a searing hot pain, shot though her. Her determination faltered. She could abandon her plan. Two blocks away she could score a bag and stop the torment. Tiffany turned to sneak out when a large black woman wearing a bright red and yellow striped caftan stepped in front of her.

"Honey child," the lady chuckled as she blocked the way with her bulk, "Don't go. I know we don't get many girls like you in here, but you're welcome to stay."

Tiffany stood mute in her short denim skirt, and thin gauzy top, not knowing what to say.

The woman looked her up and down for what seemed an eternity. "You looks a bit cold, dear. I can get you some warm soup."

Tiffany shook her head and studied the floor. "No. It's somethin' else." Most of her resolve drained away. She turned to edge around the woman. "I better go."

The woman sidled into her path and studied her closely for a moment. "Child, you best stay right here with me." She smiled and touched Tiffany's hand, giving it a quick squeeze. "I don't think you'da come in if you didn't need a bit of help. I 'spects you want a hand to pull you out. Let me take you to Pastor Andrew. He can get you what you need."

Tiffany looked at the woman with the bright sable eyes and warm smile. She knew in her heart the lady understood her plight and cared about her, maybe even loved her. She hadn't been loved in a long while.

The woman put a warm arm around Tiffany's shoulders and gave her a gentle hug. "My name's Elwina, hon. What's yours?"

"Tiff. . . Tiffany," she mumbled at the floor.

"Such a pretty name." She reached for Tiffany's thin, small hand. "Come with me. It's going to be okay, child." Elwina led her into a long hall. They passed a small chapel with an open door. Soft light illuminated a cross on the far wall and a large open Bible on an altar below it. Near the end of the passageway they stopped at a closed door. Elwina knocked gently on the dark wood.

The door opened halfway.

"Pastor, this is Tiffany. She needs our help."

A short balding man with a round face and bright green eyes opened the door wide. He wore black high top sneakers, baggy jeans and a bright yellow sweatshirt which proclaimed, 'I Love Jesus'. "Come in, Tiffany. I'm Pastor Andrew."

"Don't take too long talkin' now, Pastor. Her chills have already started."

"I'll need to call Gordie then."

Elwina grunted.

"Here, have a seat." Pastor Andrew gestured to a chair, a gang tat visible on his hand.

Before the door closed she heard Elwina say, "I'm bringin' you a mug of hot chicken soup, child."

Tiffany perched on the edge of a wooden chair beside a scarred oak desk. She looked around. No windows. Other than the desk, a few chairs, a beat-up filing cabinet, and a lone picture of Jesus, the room was bare. She tucked her short skirt down on her thighs as best she could, and kept her legs tight together. She clutched her tiny purse on her lap.

"Tiffany, you do want us to help you, don't you?"

Her lips set in a tight line, she nodded her head. "Uh-huh." Another shudder racked her body. Had she done the right thing? I hope he doesn't talk too long.

Pastor Andrew sat behind the paper-cluttered desk. A few books and an open Bible rested atop the papers.

"How many times have you been through withdrawal?"

"Twice."

"Heroin?"

She nodded.

"The treatment didn't work?"

"I was in jail."

"I see." He leaned forward, hands clasped on the desk. "They didn't send you to County?"

Tiffany shook her head.

"It'll be easier this time, but I need a commitment from you, Tiffany. Do you really want to get off. . ." He locked onto her eyes with his emerald gaze. ". . .off for good?"

She'd come this far. Do or die. She sucked in a breath and held it a long moment before exhaling. Resolve built back up. Her words came out in a torrent. "I wouldn't have come here if. . . I'll go cold turkey if I have to." She paused for a second. "I. . . I need another place to stay. Someplace safe."

Pastor Andrew nodded. "Ahhh. A boyfriend? Your pimp?"

"Uh-huh."

"You'll be safe here. He won't find you. First though, we need to help you through the next few days. We run a little clinic, and there's a doctor we can call." He picked up the phone and dialed.

There was a knock on the door and Elwina bustled through with a mug of soup. "Careful now, child. It's hot. Don't want you burning your tongue." She handed the stoneware to Tiffany who grasped it with both hands. The warmth flowed into her fingers.

"Tha. . . thank you."

"Won't take care of what's really ailing you, but I 'spects you could use some nourishment, too." Elwina ambled out the door, closing it behind her without a sound.

Tiffany took a sip of broth from the cup. She remembered a time when she was six or seven and her mother fed her chicken soup when she'd been sick with a fever. A time before her mother's boyfriend introduced her to his secret games when she was eleven.

Pastor Andrew settled the receiver in its cradle. "You can finish your soup and then I'll take you to our clinic. Gordie. . . Doc Blaisdell will be here soon. He'll probably start you on a regimen of buprenorphine. It'll ease your withdrawal symptoms. It's still going to be hard, but not as bad as before."

Tiffany took another swallow of the soup, slurping at the wide egg noodles and small chunks of white chicken. "That black lady, Elwina. She's nice."

Pastor Andrew leaned back in his chair and chuckled. "We're fortunate to have her. Her arrival was like a miracle. An answer to our prayers. She's a social worker laid off from. . . I think she said Charleston. Came here about three days ago and volunteers full time. We'll be lost when she finds a position somewhere."

Tiffany downed the last swallow of soup, shrugged off a shiver, and set the mug on the edge of the desk. "The chills are getting pretty bad. Can I go to your clinic now?"

"Come with me." Pastor Andrew led the way back out to the main entrance and through a door on the other side of the building to a small medical clinic.

Tiffany walked with him to a small waiting room, and through a warren of halls into what looked like a hospital room with two beds and three worn straight back chairs. One bed had a curtain pulled around it. There were no windows.

Elwina stepped into the room carrying a large paper grocery bag, a pair of flannel pajamas and terry cloth slippers. "I'll get her ready for Doc Blaisdell."

"Thanks. I'll be in the office if your need me."

"We'll be fine. I'm gonna get her out of her street clothes and into somethin' more comfortable. She's chillin' pretty bad already. I'll wait with her till Doc comes." She turned to Tiffany shivering on a chair. "You best change now, child. Put everythin' in this here bag, and get in these jammies. I'll pull the curtain to give you some privacy." Elwina left the paper sack on the bed beside the pajamas, stepped away and pulled the curtain around the bed. "Give me a holler when you're done."

"O. . . Okay," Tiffany said through chattering teeth. "Oh, God," she sobbed. "I don't know. . ."

Elwina hurried around the curtain and enfolded Tiffany in her arms, like a mother who had found her lost child. She rocked her gently as she said in a soft voice, "There, there, child. You and me, we'll get you through this together."

"Promise?"

"Hang with me, baby. You can do it."

Tiffany relaxed as the sudden chills ebbed. "Yes. I can do it." She set her jaw, kicked off her four inch heels and began to strip off her clothes tossing them on the bed. She took the flannel pajamas that Elwina handed her and put them on. When she finished she saw Elwina had put her clothes, her shoes and her little clutch purse with the long shoulder strap in the bag. She pulled back the covers, and crawled between the clean soft sheets.

Elwina pulled the curtain back, put the grocery sack on the closet shelf and turned to Tiffany. "You're mighty thin, girl. I 'spect you've not been eatin' too good. We'll get you over the hump here, then I'll feed you up a storm. Put some meat on them bones."

A tall, dark haired young man stood in the doorway. "Food cures a lot of things Elwina. I understand there's a patient here needs a little help." He walked to the bedside, set his doctor's bag on a chair and smiled. "I'm Doc Blaisdell, but most folks call me Gordie. You must be Tiffany?"

"Uhh-huh."

"I need to ask you a few questions, Tiffany," he said as he checked her eyes with a light. "I need some honest answers and then I'm going to give you a shot. That'll make the symptoms of your withdrawal a little easier to handle. Okay?"

Tiffany nodded.

"How old are you?"

"Turned eighteen three months ago."

He took her hand, pushed up the sleeve of her pajamas and examined her needle tracks. "How long have you been using, and how many times a day do you shoot up?"

She looked at the young doctor, then Elwina at the foot of her bed, who nodded. The doctor's touch was warm and comforting. She felt she could trust him.

"'Bout three years, I guess. I don't know how often. I wait as along as I can. Can you give me somethin', now?"

"I'm going to give you a shot." He fingered the muscle tissue on her deltoid. "We can use your arm here. See how you do. I'll check on you later and if you're tolerating the drug well. When I know it's having the effect we want I can start an IV. We'll put you on a slow drip."

"How long Doctor?"

"We'll see how you respond. Usually three, maybe four days." Gordie Blaisdell prepared a syringe, swabbed Tiffany's arm with an alcohol wipe and injected the drug. "There. I'll see you again in an hour or so."

Tiffany gave him a faint, crooked smile; the first smile she truly meant in a long while.

Elwina stepped to the side of the bed and patted her arm. "Doc might go for a bit, child, but I'm goin' to stay right here with you till you well again. Elwina's not goin' nowhere."

Chapter 11

When Tiffany woke she didn't remember where she was. Her body ached like she'd been thrown down a flight of stairs and kicked by Jahleel when she reached the bottom. Her pajamas smelled of sweat, her arms were tied to hospital bed rails and through bleary eyes she saw Elwina sitting beside the bed. Then it came to her. She'd gone to the Wayfarer's Mission to kick heroin and begin a different life.

"Mornin', child," Elwina said as she broke into a white toothed grin and chuckled, "You went through a rough patch for a couple of days. . . just out of it. How you feel? Ready for your Sunday mornin' resurrection?"

"I hurt all over and I feel weak. It's Sunday?"

Elwina looked at her watch. "Ten o'clock. Almost time for church." She put her hand on Tiffany's forehead. "No more fever. I 'spect you're done thrashin' about so we can take those restraints off." She bent to the task, first freeing the left arm, then the right.

Tiffany smiled weakly.

"Don't go movin' that left arm much yet. Gotta wait till the nurse takes your IV out. She'll be here shortly. Do you feel like eatin'?"

"Maybe a little."

"I think a bit of strawberry yogurt might be good. You like strawberries?"

Tiffany nodded.

"Be right back." Elwina bustled out the door.

When she finished the small bowl of yogurt Tiffany said, "I don't remember much. You said I went through a. . . what. . . a rough patch?"

"You did. I think you musta had more than heroin in your system."

Tiffany muttered a curse. "Jahleel," she whispered.

"That your supplier or your pimp?"

Tiffany turned her head away.

"Come on now, child. Ain't nothin' to be ashamed of. Just facts."

"Both," she murmured.

"You wanna go back?"

Tiffany set her face, and said with a force that surprised her, "No! You gotta keep him away from me."

Elwina remained calm. "Why's that?"

"He don't care. He don't care about nothing but himself and hard sex." Her voice dropped to just above a mumble. "Thinks the drugs makes the sex better for me. Really, it's for him."

"I see. We'll keep you safe here. You have Elwina's word. And we have a shelter nearby where you can live when you're ready."

She nodded. "Will I be safe from Jahleel?"

"Of course. We need to talk a little now. You feel up to it?"

Fear and uncertainty clouded her face. "Talk about what?"

"Don't go bein' afraid on me, child. You were

brave comin' here. We need to talk about gettin' you farther along the road to recovery. You're over the first hump, and it'll take your body a while to adjust. When you're through with that you need to think about joinin' a twelve step group."

"I. . . I don't know. . ."

Elwina's gaze turned to steel. Her voice took on the tone of a drill sergeant. "Do you want to stay off heroin, Tiffany?"

She nodded.

"Do you want to do more with your life than sell your body?"

A tear rolled down Tiffany's cheek. "Uh-huh."

Elwina's voice grew quiet, but it kept its stern tone. "Then I strongly suggest you join Narcotics Anonymous. Everyone in N-A has been where you been. Nobody's gonna judge you there." Elwina reached over and held Tiffany's hand. "A little help from the group, an' a little help from God, an' you can be anything you set your mind to."

"I. . . I don't—"

"Trust me, girl. You'll find people there loves you for who you are. Really loves you, like I do. Like God does. They'll be there to give you a helpin' hand when you need it." She paused a moment.

Tiffany felt Elwina peering into her soul.

"And, believe me, there'll be times when you need it."

"You're. . . you're sure?"

"Never been more sure in my life."

"What will I do? How will I live?"

"You can stay at our shelter. You'll need to take some time and figure out what you want to do with your life. I'll talk to Pastor Andrew. You're a bright girl, and you can become anything you want."

Her eyes widened. "Could I become a social worker

like you?"

"You could. But there's no need to rush. You look at me and think I walk on water. I can't do that. Settle back a bit. You got plenty of time, and Elwina'll sorta hold your hand along the way whenever I can."

It had been almost too much. "I'm tired now. Can I go back to sleep?"

"Sure, child. You rest easy."

Tiffany's eyelids fluttered, sleep tugging at them. They drifted closed. A faint smile played around the corners of her mouth.

Chapter 12

When Tiffany walked out of Pastor Andrew's office, she was surprised to see Elwina ambling toward her at the other end of the long hallway. She hadn't seen the social worker since their tearful goodbye two months earlier. Tiffany's long blond hair swung behind her as she sprinted the length of the hall and enfolded Elwina in a tight bear hug. "I'm so glad to see you, I've missed you so much."

Elwina held Tiffany at arms length and studied her. "My, my, I swear you've put on twenty pounds. And in all the right places. You are beautiful outside and inside. Your eyes are so clear now, with that pretty touch of amber around the edge. Your face glows and your hair shines. I bet your heart does, too."

Tiffany felt a flush of embarrassment, but only for a second.

Elwina let out a long chuckle. "Now don't go getting self-conscious on me. You truly are pretty as a picture."

"I feel like a new person."

"And you look like you're comin' out of your shell, too." She pulled Tiffany close in another embrace. When they broke apart she said, "I was just going to see Pastor Andrew, but he can wait. Let's find a quiet spot where we can catch up." Elwina put her ample arm around Tiffany's waist and the two walked to a small room adjacent to the chapel of devotion.

When they found seats Tiffany said, "I can't believe it. You're really back?"

"Only for a few days. Family needs me, and I gotta go take care of them. But I had to stop and see you and Pastor Andrew. Enough about me. Tell me about yourself. What all ya been doin'?"

"I'm sober. Been off heroin for almost three months now, and you were right. My group at N-A has some of the best people. They really care. Some of the guys freaked me out a little at first, but I guess that's because of the way I've looked at most men since I was a kid. And tomorrow, Elwina. . . tomorrow I start school.

"That's great. I'm proud of you."

"Pastor Andrew helped me get my GED and I'm starting college. I'm so excited."

Elwina raised one eyebrow. "Maybe a little frightened, too?"

She lowered her head and nodded. "You were only here with me a couple weeks and you know me too well." She tucked her head down. "I guess I am a little scared."

"That it'll be too hard, or that Jahleel might find you?"

Tiffany studied the floor for a long while. "If I'm honest with myself that's. . . ." She raised her head and looked in Elwina's eyes. ". . . that's something I've been working on. I guess I got to admit I'm afraid of both."

"I don't think you should worry about either one." Elwina smiled and patted her arm.

Tiffany gave her a blank look.

"God blessed you with lots of brains, girl. Don't worry. You'll do great in school, and you got way more street smarts than those other kids at college. You'll be fine. Now, I have a secret to tell you. And don't you get mad at me over what I done." Elwina smiled. "Promise?"

Tiffany felt a surge of warm affection. "I can't be mad at you for anything. You saved me. If it wasn't for you, I. . . I might be dead by now."

Elwina flashed her giant white-toothed smile that seemed to light the room and rested her hand atop Tiffany's. "You got that wrong. You were the one walked in here for help. I just held out my hand and God saved you. Now, you ready for my little secret?"

She nodded.

"When you were goin' through withdrawal I sneaked a look in that little purse of yours. Needed to find out where you come from. I got your full name and then the po-lice gave me the address from the last time they busted you. I went by to find where you lived and a little about Jahleel. I understand why you're afraid. That boy's a piece of work."

The revelation didn't surprise Tiffany. There was always more to Elwina than first appeared. "He could be nice when he wanted, but down inside he was mean. Before I came here, he seemed to have lost his energy. Complained of being tired all the time. It only seemed to make him mad."

Elwina proceeded with her story as though she hadn't been interrupted. "I kept a low profile, if you can believe it. Two days after you came here he had two new girls workin' for him."

Tiffany said, "Just like that?"

"Just like that."

"He didn't care, did he?"

"Guess not." Elwina chuckled. "Well, after that I just happened to give the po-lice some information.

Figured the law might work its magic. Today, before I come here, I checked up on him. Seems he's the one busted now. Po-lice got him for possession with intent, assault, and pimping. Those new girls turned on him. Since that's his third strike, he's gonna go away for a long, long time. He's stuck at county now, till his trial comes up. I don't think you'll have to worry about him none. None at all."

Tiffany exhaled. She hadn't realized she'd been holding her breath.

"So he's gone? Oh, wow."

"Uh-huh. Once the law brings its bar of justice down, he'll be out of your life. Don't you fret none about him bothering you."

"In a way I feel sorry for him, but I'm glad I don't have to worry."

Elwina leaned back and smiled at Tiffany. "My, my. So you're goin' to college, startin' tomorrow? Tell me, are you still interested in social work?"

"I'm not sure. I'm worried it might be too hard for me. I don't know hardly nothing that I would have learned if I'd gone to school like other kids. Pastor Andrew said the same as you; not to be afraid."

"I told you before, you've got all the smarts you need. You could be a doctor like Gordie, if you put your mind to it."

Tiffany grinned. "You really think so?"

Elwina put her arm around Tiffany's shoulders and gave a little squeeze. "Course you can. Now go get 'em."

Tiffany rose to go.

Elwina grabbed her hand. "One more thing."

"What?" Her eyes widened in surprise.

"You goin' to church, maybe readin' the Bible I left with you?"

A large grin. "Oh yeah. Of course. Read it every day. Yesterday I read this story Jesus told about this guy who went to ah. . . Jericho, I think it was, and thieves robbed him, beat him up, and left him beside the road to die. Then a guy nobody liked, a. . . um. . . a Samaritan, took care of him." She squeezed Elwina's hand. "You know, I sorta think you did that for me."

"Guess I did. Now it's your turn to find the wounded and help them. What do you think?"

"I hadn't thought of it quite like that but, you're right. I get to help those women who come to the shelter after they're beat up, or their husbands kick them out."

"You're working at the shelter?"

"Yeah." She grinned with pride. "Surprised me when Pastor Andrew asked me. Course I said yes. So the mission hired me to be a night monitor over on Sixth Street. Midnight to six. I talk to some of them when they can't sleep, or their kids are fussy. It's not a lot. I'm just a shoulder to lean on."

"Wonderful. Shoulders count, honey-child. Now, I hope you're bein' careful to get plenty of sleep. Don't want you wastin' away to nothin' again."

"Oh yeah. Don't worry. I go to bed early, and then I usually get a little nap. Speaking of my health, I got my test results back a week ago. I was so afraid I might have got infected when I was. . ."

Elwina nodded. "I understand."

"A few times, a couple years ago, I wasn't as careful as I shoulda been. The test says I'm fine. Six more months I'll get the HIV test again, but I'm not worried. I'm so happy, Elwina. I've got a whole life ahead of me. Thank you for stopping me when I wanted to run back out to the street."

"You're welcome. It does my heart good to see you growin' and learnin' God's way of sharing His love. Now, I gotta go see Pastor Andrew." Elwina rose and enfolded Tiffany in a warm hug.

As they broke apart Tiffany held onto the fingertips of one of Elwina's hands and said, "Be sure to give Pastor Andrew a phone number so we can stay in touch."

"You know I hate those things. Besides I'm always goin' to be in your heart."

Realization dawned. Her eyes misted over. "I'm going to miss you, Elwina."

"I know. I know. I'll miss bein' here and givin' you a hug. But I gotta go take care of some others." She paused, reached into a pocket hidden in her Caftan and withdrew an envelope. "Here. I want you to take this. Someone gave it to me. I know you'll find a use for it, maybe your schoolin' or helpin' someone else out."

Somehow, Tiffany knew then her fears were true. She might never see Elwina again. But a new work called. For now she'd be a shoulder. When she graduated she'd be a social worker like Elwina.

Chapter 13

In a dank alley, around the corner from the shelter, a wizened man sat on the wet pavement, his back against the wall of a building, his head bowed.

Another man stood over him. "How could you let that happen, Alderon? I swear. I give you a task. An easy one. A simple girl, hooked on heroin and you let her slip away." Heylel shook his head. "She's in our grasp and you let her go to the enemy." The man's voice took on a sterner tone. "Look at me."

Alderon raised his head. Afraid not to.

"What happened?"

"It was Paragon, Master."

"Hah. I could eat Paragon for lunch. It was your incompetence, your overconfidence, your stupidity. Haven't you learned anything? You keep floundering like this and you'll end up like Wormwood."

"What more could I have done?"

"When Paragon took the form of a likable black woman you should have entered the shelter. You could have been a sympathetic soul for Tiffany to talk to in the early days, or another prostitute who went there like she did. Then, in time, encourage her to go back on the street for the money. The heroin would have come back in due course."

"Next time I'll be more diligent."

"See that you are." Heylel stretched out a hand. "Come, now. You need to go back to work. Already Paragon is probably seeking out a new person to influence. Someone whose heart he'd like to see changed."

Alderon took the outstretched hand and rose. "Yes, Master."

Heylel looked up and down the grimy, graffiti-covered walls. "You know, Alderon, I sort of like this alley. I think I need to mark it like the gangs do. See if you can find some red paint. Two spray cans should do the job nicely."

Alderon hurried out to the street. Where would he find paint? He'd have to use his powers. He ducked back into the alley. Heylel had already gone. Alderon willed himself into another dimension and vanished from sight.

Chapter 14

Carmen Ramirez didn't know why she'd chosen the battered women's shelter run by the Wayfarer's Mission, except it was five blocks from home. But she knew, when she walked in the door at one in the morning, it must be the right place for her.

The young blonde, really not more than a girl, who greeted her held out her hand and smiled. "You're safe here. How bad are you hurt?"

"Only poquito, I think."

The young woman said, "It looks like more than a little to me."

Carmen hadn't taken the time to look at herself when Jorge left her huddled in a corner on the floor and stormed out into the night. She could move her arms and legs. She could stand and walk. Nothing hurt so bad she thought it might be broken. Nothing except her spirit, and maybe her will to live. With her tongue she felt the loose molar. One eye swollen shut so she could hardly see. She needed a place to rest and clean up. She'd be fine.

"I think maybe you should sit down," the young woman said as she pointed to a chair. "Let me get someone to give you first aid. I'm Tiffany, the night monitor."

Carmen raised a hand to her right jaw. which hurt the worst, and then looked at it with her good eye when she felt the stickiness of coagulating blood. "May. . . maybe worse than I thought." She collapsed into the nearby turquoise plastic chair.

"If you start to get dizzy put your head down. I'll have someone here to help you in just a minute," Tiffany picked up a phone and dialed a number, then spoke to someone on the line briefly. She turned to Carmen when she hung up the receiver. "Gordie, um— Doctor Blaisdell, will be here in a few minutes."

Worry clouded Carmen's face. "I can't pay."

"You won't need to. There's no charge for anything we do."

"And you're sure I'll be safe? The front door isn't locked."

"I'm positive. We leave the door unlocked for people who need help. This is like a sanctuary. I know it seems dumb, but we trust in God's protection. Nearly everyone here has been through something like you have. There are some stories you'll find hard to believe. I didn't when I first came."

"You live here?" Carmen's eyes widened.

"When I needed help I found it at the mission on Seventh. Then I came here to live."

"I thought you were a do-gooder college girl."

Tiffany ducked her head to hide a quick grin. "Far from it, although I am going to college now, so I guess in a way you're right."

"What am I interrupting?" The young man, with the tired eyes and a black satchel, said as he walked through the doorway. He looked at Carmen. "Oh, my. Let's get you to the infirmary." He stepped closer. "I'm Doctor Blaisdell. Let's see what we can do to get you in a little better shape. Can you walk?"

Carmen nodded.

"I'll need someone to assist me, Tiffany. Call Andy. Let him know what's going on. He can hold down the fort here. I'd like a woman with me in the infirmary."

Tiffany smiled and said, "Sure, Doctor. I'll be right there."

Gordie Blaisdell helped Carmen to her feet, and slowly they made their way through a maze of halls to a small infirmary. He pointed to an exam table and said, "Do you think you could sit up there?" He pulled a small step-stool to the end of the table. "I can give you a hand if you need it."

Carmen grabbed his arm and winced as she stepped on the stool and then sat on the end of the table.

Gordie sat on a rolling stool. "I don't know your name yet. . ."

"Carmen."

"Your last name, Carmen?"

"Ramirez."

"Until Tiffany comes can you tell me what happened?" He opened a drawer and pulled out a blank chart.

Carmen dropped her head. "My husband beat me," she said in a whisper, her head down.

"Once, twice or quite a bit?" Gordie Blaisdell's voice sounded so gentle. A voice of concern.

"More than once." She felt a hint of courage return. "It's worse when he gets drunk."

He wrote notes in the chart. "I see."

Tiffany rapped gently on the doorframe and stepped into the infirmary. She smiled at Carmen then turned to the doctor. "I don't know if I'll be much help. I don't know nothing about first aid stuff."

"You'll do just fine." Gordie said, then turned his attention back to his patient. "Carmen, do you think you have any broken bones, or are you just bruised from when he hit you?"

"I don't know. I don't think so. I walked here."

"How far?"

"Five or six blocks."

Gordie Blaisdell began examining Carmen. As he pushed and prodded she occasionally grimaced, but always told him to go on. She was beginning to feel almost safe, and she wasn't going to complain. When he finished the exam he said, "You're probably right. Your face is the worst. You might have a couple of cracked ribs. We'll have to get x-rays of those and your jaw tomorrow."

"I. . . I can't pay."

"You won't have to. It's all part of what we do here at Wayfarer's."

Tiffany had told her the same thing. Who were these people?

Gordie turned to Tiffany. "Could you give me a hand here while I clean her wounds, then we'll see if we need to put in a stitch or two."

"Stitches?"

"Only if you need them. I promise it won't hurt."

Tiffany held Carmen's hand and gave it a tender squeeze. "You'll be fine, Carmen. I'm going to stay with you until Gordie has you looking as good as new, and we get you settled for the night." She stopped a moment and surveyed Carmen. "Well, maybe almost as good as new."

Safe and free. Someone cared. It was a new feeling.

Gordie and Tiffany cleaned Carmen's wounds, then applied antiseptic and bandages. When they finished Gordie said, "Seems to be more bruises and abrasions than any serious lacerations, except for this one on your cheek. Let's try a butterfly bandage and we'll see what it looks like tomorrow."

Carmen said, "I don't know how I can thank you,

Doctor."

"No thanks are needed. I try to fix the body and Pastor Andrew will see if he can give you a hand at healing the soul. . . when you're ready."

"I. . . I'm Catholic. I. . . I don't know. . . "

Tiffany said, "It don't matter what religion you are. Jesus didn't care when he was here. Healing for your soul doesn't have a church. It's something God does."

"And. . . and you're sure I'm safe here." Carmen's chin began to quiver, and she felt a chill go through her body as she thought of what Jorge might do if he found her.

Tiffany said, "Oh, yes. You'll have to talk to Helen. Her husband discovered she'd come here. He wanted to kill her."

Carmen stared at Tiffany, mouth agape. "But, she's still here? He didn't hurt her?"

"Couldn't. But you'll have to have her tell you the story."

"Helen?"

"Yes. She's a tiny lady. About forty, with bright red hair. You can't miss her. Maybe you'll see her at breakfast in the morning." Tiffany helped Carmen step off the exam table. "Now let's get you settled for what's left of the night."

Chapter 15

On her third morning at the Wayfarer's shelter Carmen searched the dining hall for Tiffany. She saw her across the room in jeans and a pink knit tee with a scoop neck. Carmen set her tray next to Tiffany on the picnic-style table. Tiffany's head was bowed over her meal. Carmen waited. She hesitated after Tiffany picked up her fork, then spoke, "Good morning. It's Tiffany, right?"

Tiffany looked at her and smiled. "Yes. How are you feeling, Carmen? It looks like Doctor Blaisdell didn't have to put in any stitches."

"Better, thank you." Carmen managed a tentative smile in return. "I'm glad about the stitches. I think the worst is my cracked ribs. They hurt every time I move, and I'm probably going to lose a tooth."

"Oh, no. I'm sorry."

"I'll be fine."

"I don't want to be nosy, but has your husband come looking for you?"

"Not that I know of. I don't think he knows where I'm at. He probably went to my sister's in San Ysidro looking for me. I haven't let her know I'm here."

They ate quietly amid the bustle of others for a few minutes. Carmen pushed up her courage again and said, "Didn't you say something the other day about a little red-headed lady? Helen, I think you said. I haven't seen her."

Tiffany chuckled. "It seems I'm one of the last to know. I think it's because I go to school days and work nights. Late yesterday, when I got back from my classes I heard Helen's moving out. She's had a job for some time now, and she's going to be living in her own apartment. I'm sure with all the medical stuff you've been through, it's natural to miss some of the grapevine gossip."

"So. . . so I won't get to hear her story?"

"I think you still can. Someone told me this morning Sanjay's trying to organize a little graduation celebration for her after dinner tonight."

"So I can see her then?"

"I'm sure you will."

"Who's Sanjay. Is he one of the staff?"

"Not really, although he does help. I'm sure you'll meet him soon."

They fell silent again as Tiffany finished her breakfast and Carmen pushed the scrambled eggs around on her plate, taking an occasional tiny bite. She'd work the food around on the good side of her mouth to chew. The low noise from other conversations, and the occasional complaint from a child in the room enveloped them. When Tiffany had finished her meal Carmen said, "Could I ask you a question?"

Tiffany looked at Carmen and smiled. "Uh-huh. What?"

Carmen hung her head and stared at her half-eaten breakfast. "It's pretty personal. If you don't want to answer I'll understand."

Tiffany reached over and patted Carmen's arm.

"I've developed a thick skin. Nothing much bothers me. Ask away."

Carmen spoke just above a whisper. "You. . . you're different than the other women. And you're so young. Were you married, or. . . ?"

"You want to know how I came here? What happened to me?"

Carmen turned her head away. "Uh-huh."

Tiffany checked her watch. "I have a few minutes before I have to leave for class, so I can tell you part of my story. If you're done eating let's go somewhere quiet."

Carmen followed Tiffany to the dormitory room she shared with two other women.

Tiffany wrote a note on a post-it, stuck it to the outside of her door, then closed the door and locked it. "This'll give us a little privacy. Please have a seat." She gestured toward a chair and then climbed cross legged on her bed. "Although this is basically a shelter for women and children who have been abused, there are a few of us here who didn't come from a traditional relationship. Sanjay, who I mentioned, is one. I'm another. I ran away from home at thirteen to escape my mother's boyfriend, and lived on the streets until a man took me in. He fed me and gave me a place to stay." She took a deep breath and let it out slow. "Sometimes he would be mean to me, but the worst thing he did. . . He hooked me on drugs. To pay for them. . . . There's no gentle way to say this, Carmen. I worked as a prostitute."

Carmen sat silent through this revelation. At first she didn't know what to say. "You. . . you were. . . ?

Tiffany nodded. "Yeah. A strung-out hooker. But even then I met some kind people. I remember this one dude. Lived in our apartment building. Other than Jahleel, he's the only person I knew there. Sometimes he'd say something to make me think. It took awhile, but I knew if I didn't quit drugs and stop the way I was living I'd die from an overdose, or be killed by some guy who wanted rough sex.

Carmen leaned forward. She wondered how Tiffany came from a life of drugs and prostitution and now was so different.

"I had a couple of close scrapes. I got scared and knew I had to act. So, one night I walked into the Mission over on Seventh. I needed a fix really bad and this big black lady wouldn't let me go back outside." Tiffany paused, swallowed, then continued. "She wore this wild looking Caftan. I swear she must have found it in an African bazaar. Elwina hugged me that night and filled me with love. She kept on giving me encouragement and hugging me. The love just flowed out of her." A tear rolled down Tiffany's cheek. She wiped it away with her finger. "For three days I went through withdrawals, and the whole time she sat beside me. I called her my angel." Tears flowed now. Tiffany grabbed a tissue and wiped at her eyes then sniffed a few times. "I'm sorry I don't usually. . ."

"It's okay."

Finally a smile creased Tiffany's face. "Elwina showed me what God's love is all about. I can still hear her laugh. I can still feel her hugs. I try to be like her."

"Is that why you stayed with me when I came in all beat up?'

"Of course. It's hard for me to be open with people because of what I was before. But then I think of Elwina's love and how Jesus treated people, I. . . I can't help myself. I have to let his love flow out of me too."

"You're so different than the priests and nuns I've known. I'm sure they love God too, but here. . . you're not the same. You and Pastor Andrew and Doctor Blaisdell and the others on the staff. I. . . I know I'm not looked down on."

"This is a place of love and approval. Just like with God, you begin where you are."

"You can't believe how good that makes me feel."

"I'm glad you came here to get well. And it looks like you're healing quickly.

"When I get better, though, I don't know what I'm going to do. I don't even have my clothes. Just what I wore when I came, and this pair of jeans and a top Pastor Andrew found for me. I suppose I'll have to find work. Ten years ago I used to be a nurse's aide. Do you think I could get certified again and get a job and graduate from here like Helen with my own place?"

"If you want to. Sure."

Carmen set her face. "I know I'm not going back to my husband. I won't let Jorge beat me up again, and if I go back, he will."

"You don't have to rush. One of Pastor Andrew's rules is to let everyone grow at their own pace. I'm sure you can do whatever you set your mind to. Besides, nothing's impossible with God. And I think I can help you with your wardrobe."

Carmen felt the warmth of embarrassment creeping up her face. "I don't want to take your clothes."

"You won't. Remember Elwina who wouldn't let me go, but held onto me, and enfolded me with her love?"

"The lady in the Caftan?"

"Yeah. After Elwina left she came back once. She gave me an envelope. I haven't opened it, but I know what's inside. I can feel it. She told me to use it for my schooling or to help someone else. I don't need it for school. I have enough. You can use it for clothes."

Carmen looked down, studying the pattern on the vinyl floor. "I . . . I don't want to—"

"Nonsense. This is exactly what Elwina wanted." Tiffany hopped off the bed and opened her bottom dresser drawer. From under two pair of jeans she pulled a long white envelope. "She told me someone gave it to her. So from whoever gave it to Elwina, to me, to you. Your new clothes." She handed the envelope to Carmen.

"I. . . I can't." Carmen tried to give the envelope back.

Tiffany put her hands behind her back and shook her head. "Carmen, you must take it. You can't disappoint Elwina."

Reluctant resignation overcame her. "Well. . . ."

A knock on the door arrested their conversation.

Tiffany unlocked the door and opened it to find a middle aged woman standing there. "We're done. Sorry." She turned to Carmen. "Carmen, I'd like you to meet one of my roommates, Martha."

Martha stepped into the room and gave Carmen an appraising look.

"Martha, this is Carmen. She came here a couple of nights ago. She's still getting acquainted and hasn't met too many of us yet. I need to leave for school. Could you show her around a little?"

Martha extended her hand. "I'm glad to meet you. There's going to be a class in about ten minutes. Something about how to have an advantage in job interviews. Maybe not what you're interested in right now, but you could meet some of the other gals. You want to come?"

Carmen doubled the envelope in half and stuffed it in her pocket. "Si. I mean yes. I'll come. Thanks."

Chapter 16

Carmen sat on her bed in the waning afternoon light. She felt self conscious about the bruises and half-healed abrasions disfiguring her face. The embarrassment kept her a recluse. For a half-hour she'd been trying to decide if she should go to the celebration for Helen that evening. She considered skipping supper and the festivities afterward so she wouldn't have to show her face, but her curiosity about how Helen's husband had been turned away from an unlocked door was winning the battle raging in her mind. Sooner or later Jorge would come looking for her. What if he stomped in, grabbed her, and forced her home? She must discover how Helen had been protected. Then, too, there was all the money in the envelope.

She took a deep breath, washed her face and applied some of the cover-up her roommate, Ginger, gave her. A quick look in the mirror satisfied her. It was the best she could do for now. She found the pair of light-tinted sunglasses that Doctor Blaisdell had provided, tried to ignore her emotions, and marched to the dining hall.

Blue and red crepe paper streamers transformed the room. A thirty foot banner, made from a roll of white butcher paper with a hand-painted sign read, CONGRATULATIONS HELEN. Laughter and light-hearted conversation filled the air. Everybody seemed so happy.

Carmen felt adrift. She needed a familiar face. She searched the crowd looking for Tiffany, Ginger, or Martha; the only three residents she felt she really knew. She spotted Tiffany racing across the other side of the room, her blond ponytail bouncing behind her, then stopping by a tiny lady with flaming red hair in a pixie cut. Carmen watched them hug. It must be Helen.

She wended her way to the pair, now surrounded by half a dozen women. When Tiffany stepped back to let others greet Helen, Carmen touched her arm and said, "That's Helen?"

Tiffany nodded. "Let me introduce you."

"I have to talk to you first."

"You look worried. It's not your husband is it?"

She whispered. "No. It's the envelope you gave me."

The two moved away from the group and Tiffany leaned close. "I told you Elwina entrusted it to me." She held Carmen's hand. "I know she'd want you to have it."

"Did you know how much was there?"

Tiffany shook her head. "I never opened it, but there couldn't have been more than eighty dollars or so."

"It's a lot more than eighty dollars. I have to give some of it back."

"It doesn't matter. You keep it, Carmen."

"Tiffany, there was three hundred and thirteen dollars in there. I. . . I can't take it."

"I don't know where Elwina got it, but trust me, it's fine and it's yours."

"But. . . but. . . "

"No buts, Carmen. Elwina taught me something in the short time I knew her. When God gives you a blessing, you thank him, and then when the time is right. . . and trust me, you'll know. . . you pass the blessing to someone else." Tiffany hugged her in a tight embrace. "Enough of this about the money. Let's chase Helen down. I need to introduce you. I know she'll tell you her story."

Carmen followed in Tiffany's wake.

When the group of well-wishers thinned, Tiffany approached Helen. "Hi, Helen. I want to—"

Helen turned, her emerald eyes sparkling, and broke into a smile. "Yes, Tiff," she said in a deep contralto voice that belied her stature.

"I'd like you to meet Carmen, our newest resident." She gently nudged Carmen forward. "Sometime before you leave tonight she needs to hear about when Stan came to get you." Tiffany tilted her head sideways, "You know. . . same kind of fears. . . ."

Helen grabbed both Carmen's hands, like she'd met a lost sister, "Hi, Carmen. Stick with me, girl. This noise and confusion will die down in a bit. We'll go find a quiet corner and talk then."

"Really? It's not too—"

"Trust me. If your husband is anything like Stan, I understand. What happened to him when he came to drag me out of here some people still don't believe the first time they hear it." She looked at Carmen, studying her wounds. "Now, just stay with me, and don't worry about how you look. More than half of us here looked just like you when we came. It's nothing to be ashamed of."

The celebration ebbed and flowed, people kept wishing Helen well. For over twenty minutes Helen kept Carmen close beside her.

Pastor Andrew climbed on a small stool at one end of the room, clapped his hands for attention, made a short speech, and asked Helen to say something.

Helen stepped forward. "This party is so special. I want you to know this isn't goodbye. I promise to come back and visit. And I want to thank every one of you from the bottom of my heart. You're like my band of sisters. We've struggled and cried and laughed together. . . and in the process we've learned about love. And. . . and I promised myself I wasn't going to cry." She wiped at a tear. "I love you all so much."

When the short farewell finished she took Carmen's hand and together they walked to a corner of the dining hall, and sat side by side on one of the benches.

Carmen said, "How come everyone let you go. . . let you be alone with me?"

"They know what we're doing. You're new and they realize before I go I have to tell you my story. You know how we never lock the front door?"

"Uh-huh. It made it so easy for me to just walk in, but it worries me. My Jorge could come and start trouble and haul me home."

Helen put an arm around Carmen's shoulder. "You must have faith. I can assure you, while you're here, he won't."

How could Helen be so sure? "But the door's unlocked."

"It's always been unlocked. I had the same questions. Someone, I don't remember who, told me to read the stories in the Bible about God's protection. They told me Pastor Andrew prays and claims a promise for security every day. It works. No one has ever been hurt in here."

"It's in the Bible?"

"Of course. Do you have a Bible?"

"Tiffany gave me one. She said Elwina gave it to her."

"Ahhh. Elwina." She closed her eyes for a moment and a smile creased her face. "There was one powerful lady. I'll bet the stories are highlighted or underlined. You won't have trouble finding them. The first is about Daniel when the king tossed him in a den of lions and the other one is about Peter being set free from prison. You can find Daniel's story in the book of Daniel, chapter six. And Peter's story is in Acts, chapter twelve. Can you remember that?"

"I think so. Daniel six and Acts twelve."

"You got it, girlfriend. And if you forget, Tiff will help you."

"What happened when your husband came for you? Did he hurt you?"

"Stan couldn't even get in."

"But. . . but you said the door's always unlocked."

"It is. He came and raised a fuss outside. Stood there yelling and screaming. Said if I didn't come home he'd find a way to kill me."

"You weren't scared?"

"Oh, sure, but he stayed out there. He kept saying the soldiers wouldn't let him in. He said they wore body armor and carried assault rifles. They told him he wasn't welcome and to leave. I watched through one of the front windows. I couldn't see anyone except Stan standing out there, shaking his fists and shouting. Finally the cops came, because someone called nine-one-one. They hauled him off in a police car."

"You're not afraid he'll come back?"

"Goodness, no. Later, Pastor Andrew told me to read the promise of protection in Psalms ninety-one.

"So what did happen?"

"Oh I'm sure Stan saw armed guards alright, but they weren't human beings. I'm convinced he saw angels sent to protect me. I've never been afraid since. I read those stories every day, and just like Pastor Andrew, I claim the promise of protection in Psalms."

"I. . . I can do that, so Jorge won't hurt me?"

"You can. Believe and claim the promise. God does send his angels to guard us. He'll protect you. He'll send an angel to save you from harm. It's possible he already has. Sometimes we're not aware of what he's done."

Carmen sat, shaking her head. "Angels? Here? Really?"

"Really. Right out the front door. Promise me you'll read the stories. When you're done I think you'll believe in God's promise to keep you safe."

"Okay," Carmen mumbled.

Helen put her arm around Carmen's shoulder and gave a gentle squeeze. "I have to say a few more personal goodbyes. You'll be all right?"

"Uh-huh."

After Helen left Carmen said more to herself than aloud, "Angels?"

Chapter 17

Still feeling hesitant about meeting people, Carmen searched out a place in a far corner of the dining room at mealtime. She knew, without a doubt, the other women stared at her, probably whispered too. Two days after Helen's farewell, she watched a thin man saunter with hesitant steps down the aisle between the tables toward her. She turned her head away, hoping he'd avoid her.

A soft noise told her he'd placed his tray next to hers on the trestle table. When he sat down she realized he only had one arm.

"Hi," he said. "You're the new lady? Carmen, huh?"

She nodded ever so slightly and focused her attention on the mashed potatoes and carrots in front of her.

"My name's Sanjay. I know I talk too much. You can tell me to shut up, if you want to."

She wanted to say that, but it would be rude, and who knew what he was like. Then the name rang a bell. Tiffany had talked about him. She wondered if he'd yell at her like Jorge. Carmen stabbed at her steamed carrots. Her desire for him to be quiet grew like a tumor, consuming her thoughts.

"I'd guess you're sitting here to avoid people. And along I come and mess up your plans."

Carmen turned her head away, hoping he wouldn't notice the bruises turning yellow and purple across her cheek.

"You shouldn't worry. I've been here almost two years now. You'll look fine in another week or so. Me? I look weird all the time."

Carmen snuck a quick look. Light brown skin, large chestnut eyes, a wide smile, and salt and pepper short cropped hair. Maybe he wasn't mean after all. She had nothing to hide any longer. "You. . . you don't look weird."

"Oh, but I do. It's perception. Can't hide the fact I only have one arm." He shrugged. "What people can't see is my retinitis pigmentosa."

"Oh." Carmen remembered a little about the disease from her training years before. "So, how bad is your field of vision?"

"State says I'm legally blind."

"You don't have a white—."

"No. I didn't want to draw more attention to a second handicap, so I decided against the cane. I manage to get around. Just have to take it slow."

He seemed gentle and almost kind. Maybe just a little conversation wouldn't hurt. "You're doing well, as far as I can tell."

Silence fell between them for a moment until Sanjay broke it. "I haven't seen you at the group sessions or chapels yet."

Carmen shook her head and picked at her bowl of canned peaches.

"I'm not annoying you, am I?"

"Not really." The fellow was persistent. Did she dare? "Well, not too much."

"I've wondered why you don't mingle or talk much. It can't be just the bruises."

She slowly turned to face him. "What would I have to say?"

"I'm sure you have quite a bit to say. All kinds of thoughts in your head, just not voiced." He studied her for a moment. "I'm guessing now, but you probably said a lot once upon a time. Spoke your mind at first, but over the months and years you learned to keep quiet, especially around. . . " he paused, ". . . men."

Carmen felt the heat of embarrassment rise in her neck. She turned her head away.

"You don't have to worry about me, Carmen. You see, I was on the receiving end of the punishment, too. So, in a way I understand."

It took a few seconds of silence for Carmen to process what Sanjay told her. "You. . . you were?

"Uh-huh. My wife became possessive soon after I married, then jealous and abusive. . . a total role reversal from the stereotype. I thought I could solve the situation, but. . ." Sanjay sighed. "I was too close to the problem. One day in a rage, over an imagined slight, she took a butcher knife and tried to stab me. I tried to defend myself and she drove the blade into my right forearm."

A shiver ran up her back. Carmen couldn't help herself. She stared at Sanjay's stump. Eyes wide, she couldn't speak.

He smiled. "The end result. . . my wound developed a staph infection and the doctors had to amputate. While it healed, she framed me for unethical behavior with two of my patients and I lost my license. I—"

"Your patients?"

"I was a psychologist, Carmen. Guess I still am. Although I can't practice. At least not for money. Can't do much of anything I used to." He took a breath and let it out slowly. "I've begun writing a book though."

Writing a book? Curiosity up, she wanted to know more. "How did you come here?"

"I had to leave home. Sooner or later she would have killed me."

"Couldn't the police. . . ?"

He shook his head. "No. She claimed I attacked her, and with men usually being the aggressor. . ." he shrugged. "So I found a home at the mission on Sixth, but they have a ninety day maximum. Pastor Andrew arranged for me to stay here. It's better than the YMCA. I help out some with the therapy sessions. You should come."

"Therapy?"

"We get to talk about our problems, and how to solve them."

"Would it help me?"

"Couldn't hurt. That and the Lord's love."

A small silence developed between them.

"So you sat by me on purpose?"

He chuckled, an easy soft laugh. "Guilty. But, isn't that why most of us do something? You came to lunch today so you wouldn't be hungry. And you came to Wayfarer's to stop the beatings."

Carmen hung her head.

"I've hit a nerve. Sorry. I shouldn't push so hard. But you needn't feel bad. What you did in coming here was good. This is a place for you to heal. . . heal both the body and the spirit."

Carmen looked at Sanjay. She could tell, pushy and all, he cared. "If. . . if I went to the ther. . . therapy sessions would I have to talk to the others?"

"Only when you want to. I promise. No one will pressure you. The only thing you won't be able to stop is the out-flowing of everyone's love."

"Mmmmm."

"We meet in the back of the chapel every Tuesday

and Friday afternoon at two."

"Can I ask you something else? Ahh. . . should I call you doctor?"

"No. Not at all. Call me Sanjay. What did you want to ask?"

"Is everyone here a Christian?"

"Goodness, no. I wasn't when I came."

"Really? But you are now?"

He nodded.

"What changed?"

"I came to the realization I couldn't fix myself. Too close to that problem too. I had to let someone else. . . At first it was Andy and Gordie, then I let go . . . and let God."

"Just like that?"

"Not quite like that. I was a bit like Francis Thompson in his poem, 'The Hound of Heaven'. Pastor Andrew gave me this little book of poems. The man in the poem was so much like me. Made me think. When I arrived I didn't even believe in the supernatural. . . God if you will. I thought He was a crutch for the weak-minded and superstitious. Some of us believe easily. Some of us need a nudge. There are stories in the Bible about God opening men's eyes so they can see things."

"Really?"

"Really. I witnessed what happened to Helen's husband. Most people didn't see what I saw from a second floor window."

"What happened? What did you see?"

"An angry brute yelling curses. I guess Helen told you her story the other night when you talked with her?"

"Uh-huh."

"She told you what her husband did and said?"

Carmen nodded.

"That afternoon I saw the guards. Not many did. They were right outside the front doors, three deep. I looked down at them. Probably a hundred armed men in riot gear. No one could get in. I remarked about them to one of the ladies watching the scene play out. She stared at me like she thought I was nuts. When I looked back a second time I couldn't see them."

"So you think you saw angels?"

"I didn't know what I saw then, but the experience raised questions in my mind. I asked Andy for a Bible and began to read. The rest is history. Today, Carmen, I believe." He smiled broadly. "And I'm a servant of Christ."

"You don't tell other people this story though."

"Only when I'm led to share it. Something told me you needed to hear it." Sanjay stood. "I should go now. Please think about coming to the therapy sessions."

"I'll think about it," she whispered. Angels that appeared to some, and not to others. These people weren't like anyone she'd ever known before. She'd come for safety and healing. What else was happening to her?

Sanjay picked up his empty tray. "I'll be looking for you."

Chapter 18

After her Tuesday afternoon nursing class, Carmen decided to save her bus money so she could add to what she'd accumulated and buy Tiffany a little present for her birthday in a couple weeks. She began the fourteen block walk from the Junior College to the shelter where she'd enrolled three months earlier to update her state certification and license. Trusting in her new-found confidence, and the promise in Psalms, she no longer worried about her safety, even though her walk would take her along some of the city's mean and desolate streets. Areas ripe for crime.

With only three blocks to go she saw a gang of teens a hundred yards ahead in a tight circle tormenting a frail guy. Fists flew as they pounded on him. Even at that distance she could hear their curses. Scum. Where were the police? Those thugs needed to be stopped. She hesitated. No one was around to break up the fight. She had to act.

From somewhere inside she found strength, and mobilized like a mother bear whose cub was in danger. She ran toward the attack screaming as loud as she could. "Help! Someone call the cops. Stop hitting him."

One turned and yelled an obscene epithet at her.

"I've heard that before, you punk, and I've battled worse than you, too. Leave him alone or you'll regret it!"

The half-dozen gangbangers looked at Carmen wide-eyed as she charged them.

Carmen kept running at the thugs. Tattoos on their necks, shaved heads, pants nearly falling off. When the largest of them turn to face her, she stopped within an arm's length. "Get out of here," she screeched. Then she reached out, pulled his pants down around his ankles, and shoved him sideways. He took a swing at her, connected with nothing more than air, lost his balance, and fell into the street face first. He screamed a curse, as blood spurted from his nose.

The wail of a siren sounded in the distance. It grew closer. At last. Not long now until help came.

The remaining gangbangers gave their victim a final kick, shoved him over the curb, and ran dragging their half-naked comrade with them before they disappeared into an alley. They taunted her from the safety of their hiding place, "Gonna get you, woman. Gonna roast you for dinner."

A man yelled from a third story window. "I called the cops."

The siren sounded closer.

High up on the other side of the street another voice rang out. "You better get out of here."

Carmen took her first studied look at the victim. Sanjay. Oh, no. Bangers beating a defenseless one armed man, who could hardly see. She knelt in the filth of the gutter beside him. They'd torn his shirt nearly off. Bruises covered his face and chest. Blood ran from the corner of his mouth. When Sanjay opened his eyes she knew he was alive. "Help's coming, Sanjay. Someone called the police."

He moaned. "Oh-h-h. My ribs."

"Lay still. I'm sure the police and an ambulance will be here soon."

He twisted his head as he tried to look. "Where are—"

"They ran." Carmen gazed down the street. She saw no one in the alleyway. She didn't see anyone, not even a car passing on the street. They were alone. "I. . . I think they've gone."

Sanjay closed his eyes. He whispered through cracked and bleeding lips, "How long?"

"It should only be a few minutes." She pulled a tissue from her pant pocket and tried to wipe away the blood and dirt.

The voice from above screamed again. "Hey, lady. I told you; you better get out of there. Just leave him. He's only a bum."

Carmen looked up as a second floor window slammed shut. A lot he knew. "I'm going to stay with you, Sanjay. I'll stay 'til help comes. Don't pay any attention to the guy yelling."

The siren faded into the distance. Carmen realized then, the siren and the ambulance was for someone else. It might be a long time before the police came. She was alone with Sanjay. At any moment the gangbangers might return to kill them both. She tried to recall the words of the promises she'd read in Psalms, but only fragments flitted in her mind. I have to do something. "Oh, God," she whispered. "Please help me. Give me strength. Help me know what to do."

The voice shouted from above again. "Hey, lady! Are you an idiot? Get outta there."

"Help me," she called out. "Please." Tears and desperation clouded her voice. "Come help me."

"Not on your life, lady. Ain't safe. Get outta there."

Carmen didn't know precisely how the idea formed. She couldn't count on any help coming. She had to leave. The person who yelled from the building was probably right. It wasn't safe to stay. She didn't know how, but she'd take Sanjay with her.

Sanjay whispered, "When is. . . " It seemed he was about to slip into unconsciousness from shock. "I. . . I can't."

Carmen knew she couldn't wait any longer. "I'm going to take you to the shelter."

He mumbled something, but it was unintelligible.

She knelt close and said, "I'm going to pick you up, Sanjay. When I hug you, try to put your arm around my neck. I know it'll hurt, but you have to do it. Hold on tight." She bent close trying to grab him. "Now, Sanjay. Now. Hold on with all you've got." When she felt him encircle her neck, she wrapped her arms around his thin body and leaned back. With a strength she didn't know she possessed Carmen, pulled him to his knees, then to his feet. He didn't let out a whimper of complaint, although she knew he must be in agony. Her heart thrummed in her ears like a drum. She propped him against her, bent down again and pulled him over her shoulder in a fireman's carry, just like she'd been taught in first aid class.

First one step under the burden, then another. "Please, God," she said, "You have to help me get him home."

When Carmen staggered through the entrance to The Wayfarer's Shelter three women came to her aid before she could say a word. They helped her lay Sanjay gently on the floor. "Quick," Carmen said, "Call Gordie. And let Pastor Andrew know."

The next morning Carmen skipped her college classes so she could visit Sanjay in the infirmary. "I brought you some flowers." She placed a small vase of three white carnations next to the Bible on the table beside his bed. "Actually. . . " She looked down at the floor. "I stole them from the little garden in back, but I figure I'll be forgiven."

Sanjay let out a little chuckle.

"What did Gordie say about your injuries?"

Sanjay managed a wry smile. "I'm going to live. No serious damage. A couple of cracked ribs, a few scrapes and bruises. I'll be fine in no time. Gordie says he'll let me out of this bed tomorrow."

"That's good. I'm glad. Can I bring you a book or something to read?"

"See if you can find a book by C. S. Lewis in the library. I've read most everything, but I'd enjoy reading <u>Surprised</u> <u>By</u> <u>Joy</u> again. I think they have a large print edition."

"I'll be glad to." She paused a moment, hands clasped in front of her, twisting her fingers. "Could I ask you a dumb question, Sanjay?"

"There are no dumb questions, Carmen. I thought you'd learned that."

"I keep forgetting." The heat of embarrassment rose up her neck. "Could you tell me why, if we have protection here, and we can claim it no matter where we are, God let you get beat up by those gangbangers?"

"I don't know if my answer is correct, but it works for me. You might want to talk to Pastor Andrew. See what he says. What I believe is— God sometimes allows bad things to happen to us, so another one of his children can grow. I think you found strength and courage you never knew you had yesterday."

Carmen smiled as the realization grew.

"Just think about it, Carmen. He allowed Peter and Paul to be imprisoned. As a result, other of His children grew. We wouldn't have the book of Hebrews in the Bible if Paul hadn't been put in jail in Rome. He planned to evangelize Spain. Instead he went to his death at the hands of Nero. We don't always know the answers, but God can always bring good from it."

Carmen brightened. "I did find strength, didn't I?"

"You did, Carmen. You did. God gave you the gift

of strength, even if I had to get mugged. Now, before you go. . ." he reached for the Bible on the bedside stand. "Would you read me Psalm forty-six?"

She didn't know what to say. Eyes wide she took in Sanjay's bruised and wounded face. The Bible in his hand. "You. . . you want me to read to you?"

"Please." He held the Bible out to her.

"O. . . Okay," she said, as she took it from him.

Chapter 19

A frigid wind howled through the gullies and across the hard gray rocks of the mountain. Although Paragon looked like an ordinary man in worn, tattered clothes, he wasn't. For humans the elements would mean hypothermia. He knew he was being watched, but the enemy wouldn't come close. Not for a rendezvous like this. He sat cross-legged on the bare ground waiting, ignoring the icy blast that tore across the landscape. He knew Sophio should arrive at any moment with messages from Michael. What kept him? He continued to wait; still as one of the rocks around him. How much longer would it be?

No sound announced Sophio's arrival. A voice from behind Paragon said, "Sorry I'm late, but I was stuck in a situation."

"Stuck?" Paragon turned his head to see his angelic friend. "Not up there?"

"Oh, no. It happened before I went to get your next assignment. You know how it can be. One of those times when you can't leave."

"Serious?"

"Not in the end. The enemy finally backed off."

Paragon brightened. "Another victory for our Lord."

Sophio settled himself on the ground next to Paragon. "I haven't been able to follow your exploits, although Michael has told me bits and pieces. Looks like you're ready for the next adventure."

"Yes. I hope it's something a little different this time."

Sophio took a deep breath. "Quite different."

Paragon raised his brows and canted his head to the side. "Tell me about it."

"You'll be an old man, down on his luck."

"And, who do I concentrate on?"

"The bus driver, Miguel. You've been fortunate so far. The first three people made the right decisions." He shook his head as though amazed. "Not often that happens. We must watch over them. We don't want them to be discouraged and wander away. The enemy will continue to try and cause them to stumble, to take their eyes off our Lord."

Paragon smiled at the memory. "I'm glad. With Carmen I didn't need to become directly involved. She just needed to find the right place, the right person to show her God's love. With both Tiffany and Freddie I needed to do my work more directly— in human form."

"I heard about your appearing as Elwina."

Paragon chuckled. "That was great. It was marvelous to watch Tiffany find her inner strength, and then learning to live in the joy of God's love after she embraced His gift of life. Now, tell me how is your work going?"

"It's difficult. The war over there complicates things. There are so many to protect from bullets and bombs until they can find their way to accept the Lord's gift. And the enemy is always trying to thwart our best efforts."

Paragon shook his head. "He never quits even

though his battle is ultimately lost."

"Sometimes he succeeds in little ways, which is sad. He's still trying to take as many down with him as he can. I'll be glad, Paragon, when this battle is finished here on earth, and it can be restored for his children."

"Me, too. That'll be a glorious day."

"I understand you've begun with Miguel?" His brows raised. "Doing a little reconnoitering?"

"Not much. I rode his bus as Elwina instead of Elwin and dropped some seeds on what I hope is fertile ground. Miguel has already shut off anything Elwin says to him."

"Now, you go back as. . ." he paused, "as the victim."

"Like you did on the road to Jericho?"

"Not quite. You'll have to place yourself in danger."

Paragon nodded as he took in the information.

Sophio broke the silence. "So after Miguel, who do you want to work with next?"

"I'll have to work on Tiffany's old drug dealer and pimp. He has serious health problems. I'm worried about him."

"He's young, but the Master did say he wanted you to take care of him soon."

"I'm concerned. Bad genetics and the wrong kind of life have him suffering from a severe heart problem. I'm afraid after Miguel is shown the path to life I'm going to have to go to jail."

"Jail, huh?"

"Jahleel needs a cell-mate. I'll have to see how that works out. I'm concerned with how far he's drifted toward evil. The Enemy has him so deep into hedonism I might not be able to reach him."

"He's a difficult case. I'll think of you often."

Sophio rose and began to glow. "You will do well as always. Now, I must return to the war-zone."

"Take care my friend."

As Sophio vanished the wind died. Paragon stood, dusted off his ragged clothes, and hiked to a trail on the other side of a ridge. A trail that led him to the troubles of those he'd been charged with guarding. He wondered, as he trudged down the rocky path, if he'd be able to reach Miguel and Jahleel.

Chapter 20

Alderon met Heylel on the second floor of an abandoned building on Slausen. A late November wind chilled the air. Alderon peered out the opening where a window used to be. "See, there he is, Master. Waiting for the bus."

Heylel studied the scene on the street below. "You're right. You were smart to follow him up the mountain when he met Sophio."

"I wish I'd have been able to overhear their conversation, but you know how it is. They can see us, even if we're not visible to humans. I didn't dare get too close."

Heylel's eyebrows raised. "Paragon knew you were there?"

Alderon grimaced. "I'm positive of it. Probably knows we're here now."

A deep scowl marred Heylel's face. "I hate it. They can see us, and we can see them, except when we're behind a wall. . . or in your case on the mountain hiding on the other side of a rock or a tree."

"It doesn't seem right. Them seeing us. I despise

the advantage it gives them."

"Right now, my dear Alderon, you need to concentrate on stopping Paragon. He's been using this persona of Henry to get close to the bus driver. I have a feeling he's about to make a serious move. You'll need to find a way to counteract the power of the enemy. It shouldn't be difficult. Miguel is an easy mark."

"Oh. Here comes the bus. I'd best go."

"Be quick about it then. Remember only an incompetent, bumbling fool could fail with Miguel."

Chapter 21

Miguel pulled his city bus to the curb and flipped a switch for the doors. A lone passenger with a now familiar weathered face stepped aboard.

"Morning, Miguel."

"Sez you," Miguel grunted.

The passenger paid his fare, and slid into the empty seat behind the driver as the doors closed, and the bus moved away from the curb.

"Come on, Miguel, the sun's shining. Gonna be Thanksgiving in a few days. We're both alive and healthy." A small chuckle escaped his throat. "It's way better than the alternative. You gotta admit it's a fine morning."

Miguel growled, "Leave it alone, Henry."

Henry settled in his seat, face turned toward the window. He hummed softly to himself.

Miguel hunched over the steering wheel and wondered about Henry. What made him so cheerful this morning? Why couldn't he just leave it alone? Thanksgiving. Bah. Miguel didn't have anything to be thankful about. His wife, Felicia, diabetic. Four kids to feed and clothe. Life should be better than this.

They rode through six stops, passengers getting on and off, when Henry leaned forward and spoke again. "Can you let me off at the next corner, Miguel?"

Why did Henry want off there? It wasn't his usual stop. It was a dangerous neighborhood, but who was he to question his passenger? He obediently braked at the next corner and flipped the door switch.

Henry rose, and as he passed the driver's seat, held out a small card. "Here, Miguel. I want you to have this. It's important. Please don't throw it away." Henry turned and stepped off the bus into the fetid air of the city.

Miguel glanced at the card. A picture of a dove on a blue sky laced with clouds. A gust of wind through the open door almost tore it from his fingers. He flipped the switch for the door. Sometimes Henry struck Miguel as weird, almost a nut-case. And today stranger than usual. Miguel tempted to flip the card out the side window, instead shoved the card in his shirt pocket.

ふふんん

At the end of his shift Miguel stopped at Joe's, a legendary bar among the drivers and mechanics. It was a half block around the corner from the city bus lot. He wanted to enjoy a quick one and a laugh or two with the usual crowd. He needed something good for his day. He completely forgot the card Henry gave him. The light-hearted banter led Miguel to indulge in more than one, causing him to arrive home much later than usual.

His wife of seventeen years, Felicia, gave him a kiss on the cheek, smiled and said, "You're late. I worry when that happens. You must have had a tough day."

What now? He knew she could smell the cerveza on his breath. Would she prod and pry later?

She ushered him to the scarred kitchen table and pulled back a chair. "The kids are finishing their homework. You need to relax, Miguel. I'll give you a neck rub after dinner. Maybe you'll feel better."

He wanted her to yell at him for coming home half drunk, but she hadn't. He thought of picking a fight over something trivial, but in a moment of maturity, or clarity, knew it wouldn't do any good. Guilt welled up. "I don't deserve you, you know? You treat me too good."

"And you, my hard working husband, have too heavy a load. I know you want more, like a new TV, but the children and I. . . we're satisfied and happy. We have a roof to keep us dry. We have covers and coats to keep us warm. We have plenty of food in the cupboard. And we all love you more than we can say." She put the warm plate of rice and beans on the table. Tortillas wrapped to keep them soft lay on the side of the dish. She placed a bowl of mole poblano and a glass of horchata beside his plate. She rubbed his neck a moment. "Now, eat. You can tell me your troubles later." As she left the room she hesitated and turned. "I need to start the boys on their baths."

Miguel felt a deep ache that he couldn't describe. It gnawed at his gut. He wanted to escape, to run. . . run back to Joe's and have a couple more, or a dozen. He didn't care. The camaraderie, the war stories and the dumb jokes would wash his troubles away. Instead, he sat and stared at his mole and chicken, falling deeper and deeper into a dark hole with no bottom.

Chapter 22

Miguel lost track of the time and looked up to see his teen-age daughter, Angelica, in the doorway.

"What's the matter, Papí?"

He muttered into his plate. "Nada."

"You look so tired and worried." She walked over and stood beside him. "You've hardly touched the supper Mamá and I kept warm for you." She shot him a quick smile. "I made the mole. I started on it yesterday so you could have it tonight. You should eat some more. It's really good" She bent down and kissed his cheek, her long black hair falling against his neck. "I think Mamá's right. You work too hard for us."

"I wish I could do more for you and your brothers." He sighed and shook his head. "It's never enough." He needed to change the conversation. Angie, since she'd begun high-school, had become more and more like a grown-up. More like Felicia. Prying, poking, prodding. "Is your homework done?"

"Of course." She pulled back a chair and sat to his right. "I wish I could help more, Papí. Maybe, next year, I could get a job at the grocery store— work after school. Then I could buy my own clothes." She smiled at him. "Would that be okay?"

He wanted to tell her no. But he didn't want to discourage his only daughter. "You should study hard. Get good grades so you can go to college on a scholarship. Then you could marry a doctor or a lawyer."

She turned her head away. "Oh, Papí!"

"You know, the bus company has four scholarships a year they award to children of employees. But you must study hard, stay away from gang-banger boyfriends and drugs. It's not good mi hija."

She looked at him. Her eyes alight with promise. "Don't worry Papí. I don't hang with bad friends."

"You're a good girl, Angie. I'm proud of you." He reached over and patted her hand once, then pulled away. He cleared his throat. She's growing up. Not my little girl any longer. "Always. . . always good grades in school."

Angelica turned her face down. "Oh, Papí."

He scooted his chair back, putting some distance between them. "I'm sorry, Angie. I didn't mean. . . " He let the apology die and fell silent while he stared at his cold plate of food.

"Papí," she began, breaking the tension between them. "Can I ask you something?"

He looked at her curiously. "What?"

"Our teacher, Mrs. Dunsmuir, has given us a school assignment. It's for extra credit, but I need someone to help me."

Miguel couldn't help but smile as he remembered the pueblo village he helped her build in the fifth grade. It had been so long since she'd needed any help with a school project. "What is it?"

"It's for Social Studies. Our teacher's trying to make it like a sociology class for us so we can see different lifestyles. Then we're going to study how they became that way."

Miguel thought of the myriad lives he saw on his bus route every day. The teacher should have them ride his bus.

Her plea tumbled out. "She asked for volunteers to go to the mission downtown on Thanksgiving eve and help them in the kitchen. On Thanksgiving Day we'll help serve the people who come and wouldn't have a meal unless we helped. Could you come with me and help?"

So that's it. Like her mother she'd learned early in life to bring up the real subject later. And for Thanksgiving. Bah. Gloom clouded his voice. "What would I do?"

Angelica's voice bubbled with brightness and excitement in sharp counterpoint to his. "Wednesday night we'll peel potatoes and then Thursday we'll go back and help serve Thanksgiving dinner at the shelter. It'll be fun." She looked at him, her wide, chestnut eyes beseeching. "Please say yes, Papí. Say you'll help me."

He sucked in a deep breath. Building a pueblo would be so much easier. "Well. . . "

"Please. I already volunteered. If you don't help me, I'll have to get one of the boys in my class to—"

"You couldn't get one of the other girls?"

She looked crestfallen. "You don't want to?"

"Oh, Angie. What is your papí going to do with you? Already you have the wiles of a woman." He closed his eyes a moment. "Okay. I'll go with you. I can at least keep you safe from the unsavory elements." He paused. "Your teacher will be there?"

"Of course. Thank you, Papí." She rose and gave him another peck on the cheek then disappeared.

He stared again at the cold food and put some of the chicken in a tortilla along with a bit of rice. He took the first bite and savored the flavors. He didn't hear Felicia enter and step behind him.

She began to rub his neck and shoulders. "When you're finished I need you in the bedroom. Angelica will clean up the table when she finishes her shower." She gave him a kiss on the neck and padded from the room.

These women are up to something. Angie trapped me into helping her at the homeless shelter. Felicia didn't scold or nag when I came home late smelling of cervesa. Now she's enticing me to the bedroom with a neck rub. He looked at his watch. It wasn't time to go to bed. It couldn't be about sex. Felicia was never this obvious about making love. Miguel sensed trouble ahead. He took his time as he ate two more tortillas stuffed with the chicken and drank the horchata. Even cold the food tasted good.

Felicia turned to smile at Miguel as he opened the door. She sat on a small stool in front of the mirror brushing her hair.

"You ate?"

He nodded and closed the door behind himself.

"I'm worried about you, Miguel."

He walked to the other side of the room. "There's nothing to worry about."

She turned and shook her head. "Ah, Miguel. I have lived with you long enough to know. . . ."

"Felicia—"

"Shush, now. Let me finish. I think life is troubling you. You work hard, and we struggle. When you were young and courted me, you were full of dreams. I think you've lost them, and it weighs on you."

He sank into a chair in the corner.

"I know you love me and the children, but we are a burden. Sometimes I think it seems almost unbearable for you. You want to be strong and macho and take care of us, but it weighs you down." She fixed him with a tender look. "Tell me I am wrong, Miguel."

Silence hung between them like heavy black crepe.

Miguel hung his head. Should he admit his feelings? She knew. Felicia knew how he felt. He'd rather have an argument than this. He swallowed the lump in his throat along with his pride. "No. You are right. And I don't know what to do, Felicia. I don't know how to fix it."

"Have you ever thought you don't have to? We're happy like this. You don't have to fulfill the dreams of your youth. You don't have to be anything more than a good bus driver. I'm proud of you, Miguel. You are kind and honest. You work hard. That is enough. Now sit here on this stool and let me rub your back. Then you can take a shower."

Her strong fingers felt like heaven as they kneaded the tension from his tightened shoulders. When she finished she leaned close and kissed his cheek. "I love you. To me, you will always be my macho man."

"I should take my shower now." Miguel unbuttoned his shirt and tossed it on the bed. The card from Henry fell out of the pocket, the dove flying across the sky.

"What's this?" Felicia picked up the card.

"Oh, just something one of my passengers, gave me." He sat on the edge of the bed to remove his socks and shoes. "It's nothing."

Felicia turned the card over. "Did you look at it? Did he say anything?"

Miguel shook his head and blinked his eyes. "Oh yes, I remember now. He said I shouldn't throw it away."

"That's all?"

"All I remember. It doesn't matter." Miguel bent to the task of untying his shoes.

"You didn't read it? It might be important."

"What's to read Felicia? It's a picture."

"On the other side it says, 'God cares about you.' Then there's a Bible verse."

"Henry was a little weirder than usual today.

What's it say?"

"It's not written out. Just where to find it. Psalm thirty-four, verse eighteen. You take your shower. I'm going to look it up."

Miguel shook his head and trudged to the bathroom.

Chapter 23

On Miguel's second run for his route, Henry boarded at his usual stop. Miguel shut the door on his heels, and pulled away from the curb. He sensed, more than saw, Henry settle onto the seat behind him. He wished the man would've gone to the back of the bus, but no, Henry always took the seat behind him. Too much churned in Miguel's mind. He didn't want to deal with any of it. He especially didn't want to deal with the card Henry gave him the day before.

"Morning, Miguel."

"You're not supposed to talk to me while I'm driving." Maybe he'll shut up now. At least 'til he gets off the bus.

An accident at Wilshire and La Cienega bogged the traffic to a crawl. Miguel checked his watch. Behind schedule by almost ten minutes. He could hurry Henry off when they reached his stop. He wouldn't have to say anything about the card. He wouldn't have to tell Henry to save his platitudes for someone else. He didn't need that religious garbage. He still felt irritated with Felicia for bringing it up when she read the Bible verse to him last night. Bah. Just like the stuff about

Thanksgiving. And he still had to help Angie tonight. But a promise was a promise, even if he'd been trapped into the deal. Miguel felt proud. He was a man of his word.

Henry got off at his regular corner and said nothing, not even his usual bit about having a good day. Miguel wondered why. Maybe the guy was indeed losing it.

The day inched on, circuit after circuit through the city, until the next to the last route of the shift. A young boy on a bicycle darted out of nowhere in front of Miguel's bus. He hit the brakes and knew in an instant there was no way to avoid an accident.

Time slowed. His bus would mow down the dark haired boy, about the same age as his Juan. He couldn't stop in time. He gripped the wheel until his knuckles turned white and swerved to avoid hitting the boy. Too late. It would do no good. In the nanosecond before the bus would strike the child, Henry darted out of nowhere, grabbed the boy and bicycle together, and jumped to safety. The bus shuddered to a stop. Miguel closed his eyes and exhaled as he slumped over the steering wheel.

Miguel turned on the emergency flashers, set the brake, killed the engine, and radioed the incident to dispatch. He stood in the aisle facing the passengers. "Help is coming. Is anyone hurt?"

A lady raised her hand. "I am."

A siren wailed in the distance.

Miguel looked at the woman. No blood. Probably bumped her knee. "Paramedics will be here in a minute, ma'am."

A man in the back stood. "How do we get where we're going?"

Miguel tried to keep his voice authoritative and calm. "Another bus is coming soon. Please take your seat, sir."

Miguel turned then to survey the scene to the right of the bus. The boy's bicycle lay at the curb and the kid stood beside it. Tears streaked his face and a lady bent close trying to comfort him. Henry had vanished. Miguel looked up and down the street. No Henry. Where had the man gone?

It took over forty minutes before the police investigators, and the team from the transit authority, allowed him to go on his way— directly back to the yard. After parking his bus and filling out endless reports, he headed around the corner to Joes. Plenty of time remained before he would have to help Angie peel potatoes.

He greeted Demetrius, the bartender, and asked for his usual Tecate as he hopped onto a vacant stool at the far end of the bar. Right now he needed some solitude. When Demetrius brought him a bottle and chilled mug he poured half the beer slowly down the side of the glass to minimize the head, and took a sip. He savored the bite of cold, and tasted the bitterness of the hops. Almost heaven, but it wouldn't last long.

As mysteriously as he'd appeared earlier in the day Henry stood beside him. He slid up on the stool beside Miguel.

He expected Henry to spout some platitude, but he didn't. After a couple of minutes Miguel couldn't help himself. "What are you doing here?"

Demetrius approached and asked Henry what he wanted to drink.

"I'd like a glass of red wine if you have it. The house will be fine." Henry turned to Miguel. "Came to see you."

"Why?"

"Because I think you need my help."

"I don't need your help, or anybody else's."

"What about a couple of hours ago?"

Miguel didn't have an answer.

"Miguel, you've known me as a passenger on your bus for what now, three or four weeks?"

"I guess. So?"

"I'm worried about you."

Miguel leaned his head back and laughed. "You've got to be kidding, Henry. Hey, man, I can take care of myself."

Henry shook his head, his look somber. "I don't want to anger you, Miguel, but I don't think you're doing too good. That's why I gave you the card yesterday."

Miguel turned and stared hard at Henry as Demetrius set a small glass of wine down. He couldn't read the thoughts behind those piercing pale sapphire eyes.

Henry looked away, and put a ten dollar bill on the bar. "Keep the change, Demetrius." He took a sip of the wine, then looked back at Miguel. "Did you read it?"

Miguel grunted.

"Forgive me, Miguel. You're broken hearted. Just like the verse says, your spirit's crushed. You have more burdens than you think you can bear. God is close to you. Closer than you think. You need to let your burdens go. Doing what I do, helping those who need it, is one way." He paused. "You ought to give it a try. You could find it liberating." Henry took another swallow of the wine, slid off the stool and headed for the door.

Miguel looked at his retreating form as the bartender came to take away the half glass of wine and wipe the bar with a damp towel. "Hey, Demetrius, you know that guy?"

"Never saw him before in my life. I thought you knew him."

Miguel looked back at the exit. Henry had vanished again. It happened too fast, like when he saved the kid. Henry's appearance and disappearance seemed almost magical. What was going on?

"You want another beer, Miguel?"

"Nope. I think I've had enough."

Chapter 24

The aroma of turkey and pumpkin pie mingled with fresh-baked bread and cranberry sauce. Chatter from poor but happy people filled the air at the shelter's dining hall. Miguel kept his thoughts to himself. He'd come the night before because he'd promised Angie. Beside his wife and daughter he peeled potatoes until past eleven. He'd said he'd help her serve them, too. So here he was. He didn't feel any better for it. What did Henry know about making yourself feel good?

Angie pulled him into a room where they would receive their instructions. "Come on, Papi. It's not so bad is it?" She looked up at him, expectation in her eyes. "Look at all the people we're helping. And the potatoes we helped peel look so good."

Miguel grunted and followed his daughter. Angie worked her way to the front of the group. Just the two of them today. Felicia stayed home making a dinner of turkey stuffed with rice. He stood, arms crossed, as a giant black woman, in a ridiculous caftan, gave a short demonstration on serving the food. Didn't anyone know how to handle a spoon or a fork? Big utensils or regular size. It didn't matter.

When the woman finished her instructions she rushed around the table and enveloped a young blond girl standing to the right of the group in her arms.

Angelica stood on her tip-toes to catch a glimpse of the two greeting each other. "Papi," she said, "It's Miss Clarke. She's one of the people our teacher brought to class."

"Who?"

"Right there." She pointed to the pair. "She's studying to be a social worker. Let me introduce you." She tugged on Miguel's arm as the crowd thinned. "Come on."

"No, Angie. We need to serve food so we can go home."

She grabbed his elbow and tugged harder. "I want you to meet her. She's really cool."

Miguel rooted himself to the floor. He didn't want to talk to some college teeny-bopper even if she was going to be a social worker. He wanted to serve the food, and get out of there.

Angie raised her voice and called across the intervening space. "Miss Clarke?"

The blonde turned and looked at her.

"You came to our class, remember? Can I talk to you for a minute? And. . . and I want you to meet my father."

A broad smile lit Miss Clarke's face.

"I'm sorry," she said as she stepped closer. "I recognize your face, but I'm afraid I don't remember your name."

"Angelica Ortiz, but everyone calls me Angie. I think I might want to be a social worker like you when I get through school." She nudged her father forward. "And this is my dad."

He closed his eyes and sighed. There was no way out now.

"I'm glad to meet you Señor Ortiz. I remember

meeting your daughter when I spoke at her high school." Miss Clarke reached out and took Miguel's hand in both of hers. "My name's Tiffany and I'm afraid I'm not a social worker yet, but I must introduce you and Angie to my friend, Elwina." She turned to the woman beside her in the caftan. "Now, she is a social worker."

The black woman smiled until her eyes twinkled. "I'm so glad to meet you both." She shook their hands. "I better warn you. I only shakes hands once." She let loose with a deep laugh. "Next time you hafta get a hug from old Elwina."

Tiffany put an arm around Elwina's waist and drew her close. "You haven't been hugged 'til Elwina hugs you. I don't think I'd be here today if it wasn't for her love."

Miguel forced a smile. "I'm glad to meet you both. We have to go now. We're supposed to help serve the food." He turned away.

Elwina laid her hand on Miguel's shoulder. "Nonsense, Mr. Ortiz. We're just getting acquainted. They'll be plenty of folks to help with the food. Besides, your daughter is interested in what I do and what Tiffany will be doin' when she finishes school. Let's find us a place to sit and talk a bit." Elwina took him by the elbow, and led the way.

How did this Elwina woman all of a sudden take charge? He pulled loose and hung back as the group walked toward some metal folding chairs at the side of the room. "Angie," he whispered, "I don't want to stay and talk."

"Please, Papi. You won't have to say anything." Her warm brown eyes pled her case. "For me?"

He grumbled under his breath, but relented. Anything for his Angelica.

The minutes crept by. The two women and his Angie chattering like school kids. At last it was over.

Others had served all the food.

Glad to be going home, he pulled the car from the curb and into traffic.

Angie said, "I'm glad you stayed. Thank you, Papi."

Miguel said nothing as he drove east on Sixth Street toward Boyle Heights.

"I'm sorry I made you feel uncomfortable, Papi."

He waited a beat. "You're starting to sound like your mother."

They drove another two blocks in silence.

"Do you mean my voice, or I say the same things Mama would say?"

Miguel grunted.

"Papi it's okay to have feelings. When you feel—"

"Angelica. I'm not a woman." He glared straight ahead. "Now, that's enough."

"I know. I'm sorry. You are my Papi and sometimes when you're tired you feel grumpy. It doesn't matter, because Mama and I and the boys love you anyway. Today and last night didn't you feel a little better when you helped?"

He clenched his teeth and drove east across the river to where the highway bent to the right and became Whittier Blvd. "Where do you get these ideas?"

"You heard Tiffany and Elwina. God's love is about helping others."

"Is that where you heard it? Today?"

"No, Papi. I read it in the Bible at home, and from my teacher, Sister Beatrice."

Sister Beatrice? He'd sent her to parochial school to keep her from the wild boys, but what happened? Her mind filled with silly religious ideas. "You're going to be a nun?"

"Oh, Papi. Of course not, but helping people feels so good. You did feel better when you helped me last night, didn't you?"

He didn't answer, but he had to admit while peeling potatoes, until his fingers turned pruney, he'd forgotten his troubles. Maybe, just maybe, Angie was right—maybe helping people would lighten his burden. He didn't want to think about it, but maybe the card Henry gave him. . . . Hmmm.

He turned left on Euclid and headed home.

Chapter 25

Jahleel Williams lay on his bunk, fingers laced behind his head. He opened one eye when he heard the door clang open. The guard said nothing as he shoved a short man through the opening. The door banged shut and the lock fell into place.

The man said, "Hello."

Jahleel didn't answer.

"Look's like the top bunk's mine."

"Shut up. I'm trying to rest."

"Sorry." The man climbed on the top bunk and lay there until the call for evening chow blared over the loudspeakers.

Jahleel stirred first. When he stood, he eyed the new guy. Curly dark hair. Wide set eyes and a large nose. Skinny runt. If it came to it he could take him down with one blow. "Hey man, what is it?"

"What's, what?"

"What they got you for? I hates killers an' pedophiles."

"Don't worry. Vagrancy. Second time. Judge gave me thirty days."

Jahleel saw the telltale dirt creases in his neck. "You don't got no crib?"

The new guy shook his head. "Not right now. What do I call you?"

"Jahleel. Who you?"

The man swung himself to a sitting position on the edge of the bed. His feet dangled in the air. "You can call me Demos."

"Sounds like a dumb name to me."

Demos jumped to the floor, landing with the ease of a cat. "It's Greek." The cell door slid open with a metallic clang.

"Whatever. Let's chow up." Jahleel began a slow shuffle to the open door.

Thus began an uncomfortable relationship. Jahleel constantly looked for opportunities to stifle conversation and retreat to his bunk.

After breakfast two days later, Demos brushed his teeth at the stainless steel lavatory attached to the cell wall. He rinsed out the brush and turned to Jahleel. "I think they have a church service this morning. You going?"

"I thought by now a smart dude like you'd figured out I don't do church."

"Doesn't mean you can't start."

"I go in there with you righteous dudes, lightning come down and strike me."

"You believe God will strike you with lightening for doing what pleases Him?"

"Oh, just shut up."

"There won't be lightning. Come on. God won't kill you."

"How do you know? You hooked in or somethin'?" Jahleel stared at the ceiling.

"I've just never seen it happen. I've seen people die, but not from lightning at church. Besides it's the

118

mess hall. Can't be lightning in the mess hall. Where would we eat?" Demos stepped to the door and yelled, "Guard!" He waited for someone to come to the door. "We're going to the church service."

The guard signaled to another jailer down the corridor and the heavy barred door slid back.

Jahleel glared at Demos, but got off his bunk and followed him.

They sat in the back. The guy leading the service didn't look like a preacher. He wore baggy jeans and a yellow sweatshirt, and talked about being in a gang when he was young.

"I'd be where you are now, or maybe dead. . . if it wasn't for a miracle." He stopped, swallowed once, and took a deep breath. "And you men might not believe in miracles, but when it happens to you. . . you know. You might not have a miracle to lead you to eternal life like I did, then again, maybe you'll need one."

Jahleel muttered, "Like that's gonna happen."

The preacher said, "God knows what you need and He'll make it happen." He paused and scanned the men before him. "But you must have your eyes open and be aware. . . not shut out His Spirit. It happened to a guy once in an olive garden. Took him awhile, but he found the way." The preacher told them the story of Nicodemus and ended by saying, "The same words are true today."

Jahleel squirmed in his seat. When was the dude going to quit? He'd droned on for almost twenty minutes.

The preacher kept on. "The same words Jesus spoke to the man in the olive grove. God so loved you, that if you believe in Him, if you ask Him to be the Lord of your life, you can live with Him forever. These bars imprisoning you. . . " He gestured to the windows high up on the wall. "These bars don't matter to God. The real prison is not letting Him into your life." He stopped, bowed his head a moment, then looked up. "Now, any of you who want to talk with me just let the guard know. I'll be in the attorney's room all afternoon." He closed his Bible and walked away.

Demos turned to Jahleel. "See, I told you. No lightning."

"Yeah. Just don't expect me to go again."

Back in their cell while they waited for the noon chow call Jahleel said, "I been wondering. I knows you're in for thirty days. You never bothered to ask how—."

"I already knew. Twenty-five to life."

Jahleel raised up suddenly from his bunk, grabbed the edge of the top bed and closed his eyes while he waited for the blood to come to his head, then fixed Demos with a hard glare. "How? You don't talk to no one else."

"Don't let it get to you. When they processed me, the guard mentioned it. They're waiting for a bed to open up at Chino. When it happens they'll ship you there."

Jahleel balled his fists and glared at Demos. "That all?"

Demos shrugged. "Don't know anything more."

"He didn't tell you when?"

"Not a word, man. Just relax. When it happens, it happens. I was you I'd be more concerned about being tired all the time."

"Whatever." Jahleel lay back down on his bunk. He tried to push the conversation out of his mind, but it insisted on staying there. In his mind he called their confrontation 'the incident'.

Chapter 26

A tide of tension between the two ebbed and flowed after the incident. To Jahleel's delight Demos only pushed his thoughts and ideas so far, then he would grab a book, and retreat to silence. One afternoon, however, he went on a campaign to tell Jahleel about God's love.

The preaching ticked him off. Time to escalate. For three days, every time Demos began to say anything Jahleel would shut him off with a sharp retort.

Just after lights out on the third night Demos said sotto voce, "Jahleel, I've waited 'til now so you can't yell at me. We don't want the guards down here. You can try to ignore me, but I'm going to have my say. I'm worried about you, man."

Jahleel turned over and pulled a pillow over his head as he burrowed under the blanket. Would the guy never quit? Demos was right about one thing. With the mandatory quiet after lights out, yelling back would lead to restrictions. He didn't have the strength to fight anymore.

"Jahleel, I've been bunked with you for only two weeks. I've watched you, and in this short time I've seen you get weaker, and weaker. You're out of breath going to the mess hall."

Jahleel wanted to yell back. Think I don't know that? Instead he gritted his teeth and pulled the pillow tighter over his head.

"Something's not right. Every day you're a little worse. You can't continue on this path, man. I'll bet when you were a kid your mother wouldn't have let you get in a sorry state like this. You've got to take care of yourself. You've got to see a doctor."

Jahleel kept his mouth closed but the thoughts roared through his mind like a whirlwind. What's a doctor going to do? Make me live longer when I go to Chino. No thanks. Not like this. They gave me twenty-five to life. Looks like I won't make the twenty-five.

Demos droned on for another fifteen minutes, then shut up.

Jahleel drifted to sleep and dreamt about his mama. Dreamt about when he was a kid, and she took him to church. Dreamt about when his fever spiked to one-hundred-six, and his mama took him to the doctor. Dreamt about good times at home before he thought he found better times, and then slid into rebellion and an angry, hedonistic life. He woke before dawn covered in sweat.

After breakfast a guard came and took Demos away. An hour later he returned and lay on his bunk, but said nothing.

Before lunch the guard returned. "Williams."

Jahleel raised his head and stared at the deputy. "Yo."

"Time to go. Get your stuff." He held out a paper bag.

Demos looked up from the book he was reading. "Don't forget what I said, Jahleel. Take care of yourself. See a doctor."

Something about the way he said it caused Jahleel

to turn and look at his erstwhile cell mate. "Yeah. Whatever." He gathered his personal belongings and stuffed them in the sack, then shuffled toward the door as it opened with a solid thunk. He turned back. "What happened? You know. . . when you left this morning."

Demos's bright brown eyes fixed on Jahleel. "Preacher came to see me."

"Oh."

"I told him about you. He said he'd try to see you when you went to Chino."

Jahleel clenched his teeth, and ambled down the hall, the guard prodding him along.

Chapter 27

They shunted Jahleel into the general population when he arrived at Chino. A ward with eight non-violent felons became his new home. The large concrete cell smelled of sweat and dirty laundry, but no worse than some crack houses where he'd stayed. Jahleel didn't talk much except to negotiate a bottom bunk. He didn't think he could have crawled into an upper. He worried some about the doctor making humming noises during his cursory intake physical. All the while Demos' message of concern about his health and a promised visit by the preacher began to worm its way into the depths of his mind.

A guard stopped at the barred door to the cell. "Williams in here?" All heads swiveled his direction.

Jahleel rolled on his side and lifted his head. "Yo."

"Follow me."

He thought he was done with the process of admission. He worked his way to the door. "What now?"

The guard eyed him. "You, Jahleel Williams?"

"Yeah."

"Got a visitor. I think it's your lawyer."

He didn't have a lawyer. The dude they appointed when he got sent up wouldn't come. What now? His stomach took a flip.

The guard led him shuffling down tan cement hallways, through barred barriers in the guts of the building, until they arrived at the rooms set aside for attorneys and clients. He punched in a code to open the door, shoved Jahleel through and closed it.

The stern faced man sitting at the table wasn't a lawyer. The yellow sweatshirt betrayed his identity. The Bible on the table confirmed it.

"I don't want to see you." He turned back toward the locked door. "Guard!"

"I'm sure you don't, Jahleel. I didn't intend to come, but your cell-mate back at the county jail persuaded me to visit you. He's worried about you, more specifically your health." The preacher's voice rose to drill-instructor firmness. "Now sit. The guard isn't coming to rescue you." The preacher scooted his chair, grating it against the floor. "I won't keep you long."

Jahleel slowly turned around, pulled out a chair across the table from the preacher and slouched in it. "All right. I'm sitting. Have your say, preacher."

"You can call me Andrew. I saw Demos a few days ago, Jahleel. He's out now and came to the Wayfarer's Mission downtown." The preacher clasped his hands together over the Bible and leaned forward. "He'd asked me, the last time I visited him in jail, to see what I could do about getting you examined by a doctor. I called the medical staff here, and alerted them about you. After Demos saw me I made a call and found nothing had happened."

Jahleel wondered what planet the preacher came from.

"You're still tired all the time?"

Jahleel shrugged.

"I'll take that as a yes. I'm sure they gave you a physical exam when you came here. Did the doctor say anything?"

Jahleel didn't answer.

"Come on, Jahleel. Without any medical training I can tell you don't look well. The doctor must have said something."

"Hummed."

"So, you figure things aren't so good and they're not going to do anything about it?"

Another shrug.

"If you could get help, would you want it?"

Jahleel stared back. "Why?" Time to get this over with. "So I can live longer in this hell-hole?" He shoved his chair back and rose.

"Sit, man. I'm not done yet.

Jahleel folded his arms across his chest and glared. "Get with it then— preacher man."

"When Demos talked with me, one of our part-time employees apparently overheard some of our conversation. She asked me a few questions and walked away. Today she handed me this letter to deliver." Andrew opened the Bible and handed Jahleel a plain white envelope. "You can read it later. And yes, it's been through censorship. Now, I'm done." Andrew rose, went to the door and rapped hard three times. "Guard."

The guard opened the door and pushed his head in, "Come on Williams."

Back in his cell Jahleel lifted the unsealed flap and pulled out a single sheet of plain paper. He scanned the flowing script on the page. Impossible. Why would she? He knew her handwriting without looking for her signature at the bottom of the page.

Dear Jahleel,

I should probably hate you for what you did to me. I did once. Hated your guts and feared you'd drag me back. But I had to kick the drugs, or I'd die. The rest was easy compared to the prison heroin chained me in. I guess you're probably clean and sober now too, unless you've found a way to get your hands on some contraband. You're probably wondering why I don't hate you anymore

There's a simple reason. God's love has filled me, set me free, and changed my life. I don't fear you any longer either, and not because you're in prison. I'm not the same person you knew and I wouldn't be any good to you. I don't even know why I'm doing this, but I'm going to see what can be done so you can get well.

Don't push it away. There is so much more to live for on this side.

Sincerely,
Tiffany

Jahleel folded the letter and put it under his mattress, then lay down and let out a long breath. What would he do now? What should he do? What would happen next? What did Tiff mean about this side? He was never going to be outside. He'd die inside this concrete fortress, inside the concertina topped walls. For the first time in a long while he felt like he'd lost control, but surprisingly it didn't bother him. He fell into a troubled sleep until evening chow call.

Chapter 28

A week later the prison doctor, Fred Boggess, stood over Jahleel's bed in the infirmary. Exhausted eyes in a florid face betrayed a career at its nadir. "I'm not sure what's the matter with you, Mr. Williams. There is definitely something wrong, more than your dissolute life would warrant. The problem's with your heart, but I'm not a cardiologist. You've got me stumped." He turned and looked out through the bars of the infirmary window for a moment, sighed and turned back. "I'm going to contact an old classmate of mine in LA. Doctor Pang's one of the best cardiologists on the west coast. I'll send him the results from the stress EKG we've run here, along with your X-rays, and see what he says. That okay with you?"

"Do I have a choice, Doc?"

Fred Boggess ran a hand over his thinning hair. "Sorry to be so blunt, but it's your life."

Jahleel's breath came hard. It felt like a truck had parked on his chest, squeezing life from him. "So I can choose to just lay here. . ." He took a long labored breath. "Lay here and die?"

"We all die sometime, Mr. Williams."

"You didn't answer my question."

"No, I didn't." The doctor stroked his chin. "I don't give up easy, Mr. Williams."

"So you're going to do this no matter what I say?"

Fred Boggess bowed his head, gave an almost imperceptible nod, and walked away.

৽৽৵৵

Doctor Boggess woke Jahleel with a gentle touch on the shoulder. "I'm sorry it took so long to get your test results, Mr. Williams, but I have good news. . . and some bad news."

Jahleel blinked. Long? Only a week and a half. It didn't matter if it took a year. He wouldn't be going anywhere. "Give me the bad first."

"As you wish." The doctor opened a chart and ran his forefinger down the page. "We need to do more tests to be sure. We don't have the right equipment at the prison, but it looks like you have hypertrophic cardiomyopothy. The symptoms are all there."

"English, Doc."

"You probably have a disease of the heart that results in a thickening of the heart muscle. The short name is HCM. Sooner or later it'll kill you. If you'd been an athlete instead of a criminal you'd probably be dead by now."

"Lucky me."

"Yes, you are. Now, the good news. There are things we can do to treat you."

He grimaced at the thought. "Like what?"

"First we have to get you to a better hospital and run a couple more tests to nail down the diagnosis. I'm sending you to the state prison hospital in Los Angeles. Doctor Pang will snake a tiny catheter into your heart and measure the thickness of the heart wall. You'll be back here the next day. Then we can talk about treatment."

"Mr. Williams."

Jahleel opened his eyes and peered through a haze into a round smiling face and two intense chestnut brown eyes. He'd never felt this groggy. Some machine beeped in the background.

"Mr. Williams. Can you hear me?"

"Uh-huh."

"Good. I'm Doctor Pang. Your test went well. Touch and go a couple times while you were under. The anesthesiologist did a great job and pulled you through."

Clarity came in an instant. "Maybe he shoulda—"

"Don't think like that. Now, since we know for sure how far the disease has advanced there are things we can do. I'll be talking with Fred and advising him on your treatment." Doctor Pang looked up to the monitors at the head of the bed. "You're still coming out of the anesthesia and I think we'll have to keep you overnight. We'll be able to send you back to Chino tomorrow."

"So. . ."

"Yes, you'll live. It'll take some time to see how the treatment works so I can have a prognosis on your life-span, but for now, you're going to be fine. I'll check on you tomorrow morning before you leave."

Concern and questions ran through Jahleel's mind. What would the rest of his life be like? Stuck behind the walls until he died. The old anger flared. A volcano rumbling to life, then dissipating. He didn't have the energy. Maybe he didn't have the will.

Chapter 29

Jahleel counted it a great day when they moved him out of the infirmary and back to a cell. Away from the antiseptic smells. Away from the infernal machines that clicked and beeped all night. It wasn't that he didn't like Doc Boggess. The man was okay after you got to know him. Six weeks of drug treatment with beta blockers and anti-arrhythmic medications brought relief from the symptoms of his HCM. The medicines wouldn't keep him alive forever, but they made him feel young again. He could walk to the chow hall without getting winded.

A guard came to the door of his cell and barked down the hall. "Open eleven."

The door gave a metallic click of electro magnets parting company and began to slide open. It stopped with a sudden dull clang.

"Williams."

Jahleel sat upright on the edge of his bunk. "What now?"

"You got a visitor. Lawyer."

"Not that dude with the yellow sweatshirt is it?"

"Nope. This guy looks like a lawyer."

What lawyer? Jahleel didn't have a lawyer. The cat from the Public Defender's office who represented him when he'd been sent up didn't care. It must be a mistake. Maybe yellow shirt owned a lawyer's costume too. He'd know when he saw the face.

Jahleel stepped into the attorney client room and surveyed the small man sitting at the table. No more than a kid in a wrinkled dark suit. Long blond hair pulled tight against his head and tied in a ponytail. An open soft leather briefcase leaned against one of the table legs. "You really a lawyer?"

The man looked up at Jahleel with piercing blue eyes. "Sit down, Mister Williams. I don't have a lot of time today. I need to be in court in an hour and a half. It's a long drive back to the city. And in answer to your question. Yes, I'm a lawyer. Name's Neil Johnston. I work for a legal aid firm and I'm here because I promised someone I'd look into your case."

"Who that be?"

"Privileged information, Mister Williams. I'll ask the questions. Now, sit down so we can get to business."

Jahleel sat.

Johnston pulled a thin folder from his briefcase. He flipped through a few pages, then closed the file. "As I understand it, they sentenced you under the three strikes law. Correct?"

Irritation flared. "Yes, but I—"

"We'll get to your story in a minute. I need to verify some issues and events."

Jahleel gritted his teeth. Who was this dude? Who sent him? At least he seemed more interested from the get-go than the public defender cat. Jahleel decided he didn't have much choice but to go along, at least for awhile. "What you want to know?"

"It seems your first conviction was for pimping,

correct?"

"Yeah."

"And your second conviction. . ." He checked the folder again. "Drug possession which they prosecuted as a felony because of your past record?"

"Yeah. That's what sucks, man."

"And your third? Drugs again?"

"Yeah. Sent me up for good because of a dime bag."

"Any more arrests?"

Jahleel let out a little snort. "Yeah. But I always beat it."

"So, you've got an extensive criminal history; a rap sheet long enough to choke on, and you think you got a raw deal?"

"That's 'bout it."

"I have no idea why someone wants me to help you, but I want to find out. There are a couple of things we could try to work on. I'll see you in a week." Neil Johnston stuffed the file in his case, went to the door and called for the guard.

Jahleel wondered what couple of things the little twerp could work on, but the skinny lawyer didn't give him a chance. Didn't listen to his story much either.

When Jahleel started to ask, the lawyer-dude cut him off, "Like I said, I'll see you next week."

Back in his cell, Jahleel lay on his bunk and wondered what kind of lawyer this Johnston cat could be. The days stretched to a week, then a week and a half, then another day. He spent the hours lying in his bunk, staring at the ceiling. He knew exactly how many pimples and chips there were in the paint. Johnston hadn't come back like he promised. Same old, same old. Lawyers were liars. When his cell mate asked what bugged him, Jahleel told him to shut up.

By day thirteen he didn't care. He turned his head and looked when he heard the guard yell down the corridor, "Open eleven." The locks clicked and the door rolled open. "Williams. Your lawyer's back."

Jahleel stepped into the austere room with tan painted concrete walls. A table and two chairs occupied the middle. The janitor crew had been there and left the aroma of industrial strength pine cleaner hanging in the air.

Neil Johnston sat in the far chair, a soft sided briefcase on the floor. He smiled a thin smile when Jahleel entered. "Have a seat."

"'Bout time. I thought you'd quit."

"Sorry." Johnston took a breath and let it out. "I had a funeral to attend."

"Oh." Maybe the guy wasn't so bad.

"In my research about your case, and study of precedent I've—"

"Who died?"

Neil blew out a breath and leaned back in his chair. "A relative. Now can we get back to you?"

"You mean you found something?"

"I did. I think you'll like it. It involves section 17-B of the California Penal Code. Usually its function is to have misdemeanors reclassified as felonies." He paused. "But it can go the other way, too. I think we've got half a shot at getting your second conviction reduced to a misdemeanor. You'd have to keep yourself clean from now on. . . or you'd end right back here."

Jahleel's eyes widened. "Why are you doin' this?"

"Did you hear what I said about not breaking the law? And no, I'm not going to say. Like I told you last time. Someone asked me to."

The preacher? Nah. Demos? I doubt it. Tiff? Not in a million years. "An' you're not tellin'. Right?" Jahleel stopped and leaned forward until he was ten inches from Johnston's face. "And yes, lawyer man, I heard you. We get there. . . Judge is goin' to say the same thing. I get the message loud and clear."

Neil nodded.

Jahleel leaned back in his chair. "You know. I been thinking. You're a pretty smart cat. You could be drawin' big bucks working for some high priced city firm. Why you doin' legal aid? Why not work for the public defender? You're way better than the lazy so-and-so got me sent up."

"Thanks for the compliment. I do this because I saw too much of the wrong way. Too much greed. Too many people who don't care. The one person I knew who really cared was my grandmother." He stopped, swallowed once, and took a breath. "Now she's gone."

"The funeral you went to. Hers?"

"Yeah. I think we're done for today, Mr. Williams. I'll have to file motions with the court, and they should move you back to county lock-up before too long." Neil Johnston stood, picked up his briefcase, and called for the guard to let him out.

Chapter 30

Jorge Ramirez reeked of cheap Tequila when he stumbled, unshaven and dirty, into the women's shelter on Sixth late at night. "I want my woman. Where do you have her?"

"There's no need to shout, sir," said the slight, one armed man with short cropped, graying hair who sat behind a small table. "Please sit here and tell me who you want to see."

Jorge slammed his fist down on the scarred table as he shouted a curse. "Where's Carmen? She has to be here."

The man smiled. "Why do you say that?"

Jorge knew in his heart he'd come to the right place. He must find his Carmen. He wanted to grab the skinny imbécil pequeño by the throat and shake the information from him, but he knew if he did somebody would call the cops. He balled both beefy fists and leaned forward into the guy's face. "Tell me where she is. Now!"

"Sir. Before I can help you, you'll have to sit down." The thin man wiped the spittle from his face.

Jorge glared at the man.

"I'm sorry, sir. There's no one named Carmen here." He smiled again and gestured to the empty chair. "I understand how frustrating it can be when you can't find someone. If you'll sit here and tell me a little about her maybe I can help you. We have people come here all the time, and then they leave."

He knew the man was lying. He leaned forward and glared. "Why are you hiding her? I know she's here." He turned from the desk and took two steps farther into the building, then stopped abruptly. Where did the armed guards come from? One minute it was him and the skinny man, then in a flash two burly men blocked his way. They didn't say anything, but Jorge couldn't hold their gaze. It seemed they looked right through him. He knew he'd had too much to drink, but this was no mirage, no trick of his imagination. He glanced back at the man at the desk who seemed oblivious to the scene.

The man motioned him back. "Come on, sir. Sit down. Tell me about Carmen."

Jorge looked from the men standing like sentries, their weapons at the ready, to the man at the desk and backed with cautious steps to the chair. "Who. . .who are? Where did those guys come from?"

"We have protection you wouldn't understand." A wry smile lit the man's face. "I can assure you they won't hurt you as long as you stay here with me. Now, please tell me, how long have you searched for her?"

"What. . . what's going on? Who. . . who are you? I thought this was a shelter for women."

"My name's Sanjay. I stay here and sometimes, like tonight, do duty on the front desk. You said you wanted to find a lady named Carmen?"

Finally, what he'd come for. He focused through his inebriated haze. "Yes. Is she here?"

Sanjay shook his head. "No one named Carmen is living here. I'm sorry. Why'd you think you'd find her here?"

He cast a glance at the guards. Still there. "She has to be. I've looked everywhere else."

"Everywhere?"

"Yes. At her sister's down in San Ysidro, at the Union mission, and at the mission over on Seventh. All the shelters. Everywhere I could think of. I thought maybe she'd come back home." He closed his eyes and shook his head. "Now I've lost my job and been kicked out of our apartment. . . " Jorge let his lament drift to nothing.

"I'm sorry. How long have you been looking for her?"

"It doesn't matter."

Sanjay leaned forward and caught Jorge's gaze. "It always matters."

He felt this guy cared. Maybe all wasn't lost. Jorge held his swarthy chin in a meaty hand. "I dunno. I guess about five months. Maybe six."

"Have you filed a missing person's report with the police?"

Jorge hung his head. "Uh, no."

"You should. Maybe they could help."

"They'd ask too many questions."

Sanjay let the air hang empty between them for a few moments. "I take it things weren't good when she left?"

Jorge shook his head.

"I see."

"I swear, we only had an argument. Just a little disagreement. She was fine when I walked out."

Sanjay held Jorge's look before he spoke. "Are you sure?"

He remembered Carmen curled in a heap on the floor, her face bloody. "I know she was alive. This is just like the cops would ask. Everybody thinks I did something to her."

"My apologies for offending you."

Jorge noticed the guards had gone and decided to push it with this Sanjay guy. His head began to clear. He marveled that fright could make you sober. He stared into Sanjay's large chestnut eyes. "Was my Carmen ever here?"

Sanjay tilted his head sideways and smiled. "I don't know if it was the lady you've referred to, but someone named Carmen stayed here for a short time." He paused. "Months ago, now."

"I knew it! Where is she?"

"She's gone now, and I don't know where she is. She might not even be the Carmen you're looking for."

Jorge took a deep breath and let it out slowly. "I should have come here first. I didn't because it's close to where we lived. I thought she'd go far away."

"It might not be the same person. There are a lot of Carmens in the world. I think you should talk with our director, Pastor Andrew. He might know more. Can you come back tomorrow at noon? He's usually here then."

Jorge nodded. A glimmer of hope glowed within. It wouldn't be so cold tonight at his camp under the freeway overpass.

Chapter 31

The first rain of the season, bolstered by a tropical storm churning up the coast of Baja, drenched Jorge by the time he arrived at the shelter. His dark untrimmed hair lay plastered against his skull and dripped rivulets down his neck. He didn't have a watch, but his stomach told him it was well past noon. He tried to shake the water off as he stepped inside the Wayfarer's shelter.

A gringo woman, who looked to be in her forties, glanced up from a book as he walked in. She smiled and tucked a stray strand of brunette hair behind her ear. "Can I help you?"

He lowered his voice, trying to sound important. "I came to see the director. The man I saw last night told me his name." Jorge closed his eyes momentarily. "Umm. I think he said Mr. Andrew."

"Oh yes. Sanjay left a note here. Let me call Pastor Andrew. I believe he's expecting you." She picked up the phone. "It'll just be a moment. Please have a seat."

This was so different from the night before when the guards appeared and blocked his way. Now, it seemed this woman welcomed him. Could it be a trap? He'd find out what the people here were like soon enough when he talked to this Andrew dude.

"Hello there," said the man in the yellow sweatshirt and baggy jeans. "I'm Pastor Andrew." He smiled. "I understand you're looking for someone."

Jorge studied the man for a minute. The shiny bald head, and grey bushy eyebrows meant he had to be older. Jorge calculated he could intimidate this guy if he needed to. No threat there. The only question left was what to do if the guards showed up again. "Umm, yeah."

"Follow me." Pastor Andrew turned and led Jorge through the doorway where the guards stopped him the night before.

Jorge's wet shoes squished as he followed Andrew down a hall and into a bright office. Books and papers cluttered the scarred desk inside.

"Have a seat. Don't worry about getting the chair wet."

Jorge sat on the front edge of the chair refusing to let his teeth chatter.

Pastor Andrew smiled, his intense green eyes twinkling. "So tell me, what's your name and who are you looking for?

"Ahhh. . . Are the guards from last night still around?"

Pastor Andrew chuckled deep inside his throat through closed lips. "I heard about your encounter. They're always here. You might not see them right now, but they're close." Another chuckle escaped as he leaned forward on his desk, hands clasped in front of him. "I don't think you have anything to fear, though." His chair emitted a squeak as Andrew settled back. "So tell me who you are, and who you're looking for."

"My name's Jorge and I'm looking for my wom—ahh, my wife. "Her name's Carmen. Carmen Ramirez. Is she here?"

"You must understand, Jorge. The people who come

here, come for refuge. I'm afraid I must be blunt. When a husband comes looking for his mate, they usually want to take them home, and whatever drove the women here begins again. We exist to provide a refuge for those who come seeking solace and a new life. No one should have to endure abuse. It doesn't matter if it's physical, verbal, or emotional. When abuse is inflicted it wounds the body and the soul. That's not the Lord's way. Relationships should be based on love and trust. So, from what I see and hear you say, Jorge, I'm afraid I can't help you find Carmen."

Jorge sucked in a deep breath and held it until he had the disappointment and anger under control. "I really thought last night she was here. If it wasn't for your guards I'd have looked all through this place until I found her."

Pastor Andrew shook his head. "I'm sorry, Mr. Ramirez. She's not here. Many women over the years named Carmen have stayed here, but there's no one named Carmen here now." Pastor Andrew took a deep breath and let it out slowly. "I don't know if it will do any good, but you might file a missing person's report with the police."

"The little man in front told me the same thing last night."

"And you don't want to, because?"

Jorge hung his head and shook it slowly. "There's no other way? I've looked everywhere. I want her."

"Carmen isn't yours to possess, Jorge. While it's possible one of the women named Carmen who've passed through here is your wife, if she'd wanted to return, don't you think she would?

Jorge lowered his head and nodded assent.

"We don't own people, Jorge. We don't force people to do our bidding. That's nothing more than slavery. And like I said, it's not God's way. We're all his children, learning and growing together in love."

Andrew paused. "There's one other way in which you might be able to find Carmen."

Jorge's head bobbed up. Hope rose and lit his eyes. "Yes?"

"You might not like what you hear."

"Anything." He waited a beat. "Well, except the police."

"This doesn't have anything to do with the police."

Jorge relaxed. Maybe there was a chance.

"Can I be candid with you, Jorge?"

Anything to get his Carmen. "Sí." His head bobbed up and down. "Of course."

"I've watched you as we talked. Your expressions have told me a lot about you, Jorge."

"You can't know." Jorge felt a flush creep up his neck and into his face. He clenched his fists until his nails dug into his palms.

"Oh, but I do. Not as much as Sanjay learned last night, but enough to confirm his conclusions. I'm thinking you don't want to file a police report because you—."

"How?" This old man knew something. The anger burned within. He clenched his teeth. "How do you know?"

A wry smile creased Andrew's face. "Sanjay is a psychologist. He reads people very well, and he gave me a report of your visit."

"Oh." A shrink? This wasn't going as well as he wanted.

"So you don't want to file a missing person's report for Carmen with the police because in the past you've been abusive, and you're afraid of the questions they might ask."

Jorge swallowed, but said nothing.

"So what you need to do. . . " Andrew waited a beat, "is to have God bring Carmen back to you."

His eyes widened. All interest now. "He'd do that?"

"I don't know. It's up to God, and you, and Carmen. The reason Carmen left is because you made her life a living hell. You'd have to change, Jorge. Really change. I know of only one way."

Brows furrowed. "How?"

"You must let the Lord take all the hate and anger out of your life and replace it with his love. You have to decide to let God have his way in your life twenty-four seven." Andrew leaned forward, hands clasped in front of him. He fixed Jorge with an unrelenting gaze. "Do you want to do that?"

This Andrew preacher guy reminded Jorge of the guards the night before. He took a deep breath. He couldn't count the times he'd been sorry after beating Carmen. Street fights were different. You needed to live with a quick fist to survive. "I've tried to change before. Doesn't work."

"Have you've ever tried to let God change you?"

Jorge studied the floor for a long while, then stared at Pastor Andrew.

"I sense you're not ready to do it now, either." A long pause from the yellow-shirted preacher. Another steely gaze. "Not yet. And I can't do it for you. This must be your decision, Jorge. I want you to take this little booklet. It's a part of the Bible; the book of John. I've marked some passages near the end in chapter eighteen. You'll find a man named Peter with a quick temper, very much like you. Read it and come back to see me when you're ready to invite God to change your heart. My card is inside with my phone number. I'll be waiting for you."

Chapter 32

Jorge made his way back to the Wayfarer's shelter one night three weeks later. This time he didn't reek of Tequila, but he hadn't called Andrew either. When he walked in he saw the skinny Indian inside. He smiled as he said, "Hello."

A flash of recognition lit Sanjay's face. "Back again?"

"Yes. I wanted—"

"I'm sorry. It's late, and Pastor Andrew isn't here."

"I. . . I didn't want to see him. I hoped you'd be here."

Sanjay's eyes widened. "Me? I'm afraid I can't do much for you. Have you found. . . ." Sanjay closed his eyes a moment. "umm. . . Carmen?"

"No, I haven't. I came back the next day and talked with the director. He gave me a little book. Told me to read it." Jorge pulled a small, well-thumbed booklet from his jacket pocket. "I have questions. I wanted to talk to you."

Sanjay eyed the book. "Ahh. It looks like Pastor Andrew gave you the book of John. You've read it?"

Jorge nodded.

"Did he mark any places for you?"

Jorge hung his head. "Sí. I found myself there. I guess I'm a lot like the man called Peter. He used a sword instead of his fist, but to me it's the same thing."

"You're right, but why did you want to talk to me instead of Pastor Andrew?"

Jorge's mouth took on a hard look, and a frown marred his forehead. "You can't tell him."

"If that's what you wish. I promise I won't."

"Honest? Shrinks don't tell?"

"Honest."

I'd rather talk with you because you seem kinder. That preacher, Mr. Andrew. . ." He studied the floor for a moment. "The things he said." Jorge sucked in a breath. "They hurt like he'd nailed me with a right hook. Nobody's talked to me like that since I was a kid."

"So you thought I'd be a little kinder to you?" A smile flitted across Sanjay's dark face. "No body blows?"

Jorge nodded. The guy had a sense of humor. A chuckle escaped. "He told me you were a shrink, and I know you guys sorta know what goes on, but I swear Mr. Andrew could read my thoughts."

Sanjay leaned forward. "So, what's on your mind?"

Jorge drew a deep breath. "He told me I needed to let God take the anger from me. I just don't see. . ." His words drifted off.

"Tell me, Jorge, do you believe in the existence of God and the devil?"

"Of course, and the Holy Mother too, but. . . but I haven't been to confession since. . ." he thought a minute. "I guess I was around thirteen."

"No matter. God dwells on a different plane than us. He has more power than you can imagine, and he can change you."

"What do you mean?"

"You've read the little book Pastor Andrew gave you?"

"Many times."

"All of it?"

He nodded vigorously. "Sí."

"Near the beginning, Jorge, there's a story about a man who came to Jesus in the middle of the night. Christ told him he needed to be born again. He needed to have a change of heart." Sanjay held out his hand and took the booklet, then turned to the story of Nicodemus. "Here, read this again." He waited while Jorge's finger traced the words on the page. "I was once much like you, only I used my words instead of my fists. Christ changed me. He can take the anger and hurt from your heart."

"I remember the story, but I didn't understand it. Why did he come to Jesus?"

"Because he was like you. He needed to change. Nicodemus wanted eternal life in God's kingdom. The question you need to ask yourself is, if you want to change."

Jorge brightened. "I do. Now, I can get my Carmen back."

"Not quite, Jorge. We don't let Jesus into our lives to get what we want. We let him into our lives so he can fill us. When he lives in us, we'll be changed. We don't always get what we think we want."

"You mean I might not get my Carmen?"

"Whether Carmen comes back is up to God, and how he works in your life, and hers. There are no guarantees, Jorge. The only promise we have is eternal life." He paused. "That alone is enough."

This wasn't what he wanted to hear. "But. . . but Andrew told me. . ."

Sanjay shook his head. "Perhaps, Jorge, you heard what you wanted to hear."

Jorge threw the worn copy of John's gospel on the table. "Enough! No more." He stormed out into the night slamming the door and muttering curses. He'd find a liquor store and buy a bottle of tequila, then hole up in his hiding spot under the freeway.

At the bodega Jorge fished in his pocket for his last coins. He counted them out. Still seventy-eight cents short for the cheapest bottle of tequila. He was about to scoop up the money he'd put on the counter and leave when an old woman walked up and stood beside him.

"Looks like you need some help, senor."

Jorge stared at her. "What?"

The woman pulled a dollar from her purse and placed it on the counter. "Hate to see a man suffer." She gave him a quick smile, then turned and walked away.

Jorge wasn't about to refuse. He shoved the money across the counter to the store-keeper, grabbed the sack with his bottle of tequila, and left the bodega.

Chapter 33

The old woman followed Jorge down the street, tailing him half a block behind. She felt good about the way she'd trapped her prey. Jorge showed all the signs of anger and self-pity. The Tequila would put him over the edge.

"Pssst." The sound came from an alley.

She turned. A form in the shadows. Afraid of no human, she stopped and looked. She wasn't surprised. Heylel. "Master. You saw?"

"Yes, Alderon. I did. You're learning. Disguising yourself as those in the enemy camp do. The old lady disguise. Pure genius. I commend you. And then to give him the money. You should be proud of yourself. Almost makes up for your earlier failures." A small puff of air, like from a child's balloon, and Heylel vanished.

Alderon smiled. Yes, the ploy had been genius. When she looked out on the street she'd lost sight of Jorge, but it didn't matter. Tonight the man would drink himself into oblivion.

Chapter 34

Jorge clenched the paper bag containing a quart of tequila in his right hand. He took another swig, and then caught sight of the freeway overpass marking his home. He scanned the nearly deserted street that passed under the Santa Monica Freeway. Half a block later he lifted the mouth of the bottle to his lips again and felt the pale amber liquid burn down his throat. Time to climb the concrete slab to his home. Twice he stumbled and fell clambering up the cold, steep apron before he reached his hidey hole right under the thundering traffic. A night of stoned out sleep and he'd be ready to hold up his sign on a street corner or freeway ramp in the morning.

A man slept in his space. "Hey! Whatcha think you're doing? That's my place. Get out." He grabbed him by the front of his jacket and yanked the guy upright. The ambient glow of a passing car on the street below illuminated the face. He'd seen this jerk before. He stood face to face with Elwin, who'd lived on the floor above him in the apartment building. The meddlesome dude he'd punched out. He'd have to slug him again. "Get out of here. Find your own place," he screamed spraying spittle at the intruder.

Elwin held his arms up to fend off the blows. "Okay. Okay. I'm going."

Jorge released his hold on the coat and aimed for Elwin's gut with a hard right jab.

Elwin grunted then doubled forward. "No. Please. I'll go."

Jorge grabbed him by the throat, planted his feet, and threw Elwin back against the concrete abutment. He heard a hollow crack like a melon being dropped on the ground. Elwin didn't even cry out in pain. Jorge pulled the limp body forward, and let it roll down the steep concrete to the road below. The outline of the form lay motionless on the asphalt. He held his trembling hands to his face "Holy Mother of God, what have I done?" His heart hammered in his chest.

As quick as he could Jorge crawled behind a concrete buttress to hide himself from the view of any car that might drive down the street. There wasn't time to escape. He'd been in many fights. He'd hit people and spilled their blood. Sometimes a lot, but he'd never killed a man before. His fists and quick anger, just like Peter's, shoved him to the edge of ruin. If anyone saw him. If anyone called the cops. He refused to think of the consequences.

He wedged himself into a tiny ball behind the cold pillar and watched to see what would happen. And he prayed for a miracle. A miracle to save him from being caught and hauled off to jail.

A moment later, but to Jorge it seemed like an eternity, a car pulled to the curb. The driver put on his emergency flashers. Jorge peeked around the column. His heart thudded at a rapid pace in his ears. A man and a woman got out and bent down to examine Elwin's still form. Jorge could see the man calling someone from his cell phone. Then came the sirens and the ambulance and the police with blazing red lights. When the police flashed their lights around Jorge squeezed his body further into the cleft, and hoped they wouldn't see him. Hoped they wouldn't climb the concrete slope hunting. He stayed huddled in a tight ball, shivering in the night air until the emergency beacons quit flashing, and he heard the vehicles drive away.

Sober now, he lay down, but his gut churned and sleep refused to come for hours. What could he do to rid himself of the guilt? Tomorrow, he vowed, he'd go to a homeless shelter, one of the city's many missions. He'd get cleaned up, find a church, and confess his sin. He knew the priest would absolve him. Then, after confession, he thought he'd feel better.

Chapter 35

The noise of the cars rolling by as people went to work woke Jorge to a world of pain. The worst hangover he could remember. He fumbled for the tequila bottle. Empty. He didn't remember drinking the rest last night. He did remember what he needed to do. He looked down the stretch of concrete to the street below. The faint trail of dark stains on the cement confirmed what happened hadn't been a bad dream. He gathered his bedroll, his cardboard sign, and in a rare rational moment the empty tequila bottle. He didn't want to leave his fingerprints. He couldn't stay here another night. With daylight the police might return. His belongings held tight in his arms, Jorge scooted down the forty degree slope of concrete to the road.

He steadied himself for a few moments, squinting in pain against the sunlight as he tried to remember what direction to go before he began a painful shuffle to the Union Rescue Mission. Each step jarred something sharp in his head. After two blocks he found a trash dumpster and threw his smelly bedroll, the empty bottle, and sign inside. After a week or so at the Union Mission he'd steal another bedroll and make another sign. He needed a shower and absolution, then life could go on.

He hobbled west on Venice 'til it became Sixteenth, the cars on the freeway rumbling by above him. He turned north on San Pedro. Another mile or so to go. The traffic noise faded. Past the industrial buildings and parking lots he trudged, 'til he crossed Sixth Street.

As he stepped inside the shelter he knew he looked like a wrecked bum. Smelled like one too. They'd take care of him. They'd give him what he needed. In a week or so he could get a job and hunt for his Carmen again. Find her. Drag her home where she belonged.

A man with a sharp face and salt and pepper hair cut short stopped him three feet inside. "I'm sorry sir. We've quit serving breakfast."

While Jorge needed food the very thought of something hitting his stomach sent waves of nausea through him. "I. . . I just need a shower."

"I'm sorry there too. We're out of room. No beds. We filled up last night. You could try again early this afternoon. Some will probably move on."

His immediate reaction was to ball his fists, but he remembered where that took him. "I really need a shower."

"I can see that." The man pushed his chair back and turned his head. "There are some other places within a few blocks. If you don't want to wait for a space to open up here, you could try them." He bent down to pick up some papers in an act of dismissal.

Jorge sucked in a deep breath, turned and walked out into the brisk morning air. He looked up at a few pale wisps of cloud. Strands of flowing white hair painted across the azure sky. The beauty meant nothing. He started walking with no specific place to go. He'd try every shelter he came to. Someone would have a bed and a shower.

To his fogged mind the entrance looked familiar in a vague sort of way, but he couldn't place it. He opened the door and stepped inside without paying attention to the sign.

"Hello, Jorge. I've been expecting you."

He couldn't speak. He'd seen the man die. He'd heard the crack of bone. He'd watched the body lie on the road, inert, until the ambulance hauled it away. In the morning he'd seen the trail of blood. "Ahh. . ."

Elwin Hunter stared at Jorge with a penetrating look, like the guards stared at him the first time he'd come here. "It's all right. I know it's a shock, but God needed to do something to get through to you."

Jorge stared at Elwin. Color drained from his face. "I. . ."

"Yes, you hit me. And no, you didn't kill me. For now, let's just chalk it up to a small miracle. After your shower. . ." Elwin skewered Jorge with his gaze. "You and I are going to talk."

Jorge felt sweat run down his sides. "Ahh. . . Why?"

"Because, Jorge, you are precious to the Lord. It's time to quit running away from him. Time to let him take away your anger. Now come with me. Let's get you some clean clothes and a shower."

For the first time in weeks Jorge felt refreshed. No more grime. No more sweaty smell. They'd given him a bed in a room with his own bath and new clothes. Chinos, a dark blue polo shirt, and new sneakers. On the table beside his bed he found a glass of cold milk and two soft chocolate chip cookies. He took a bite, savored the sweetness of the brown sugar, the bite of dark chocolate. When he finished he picked up the crumbs with his fingers and ate them, too. When he stepped out of the room he found Elwin in the hallway, sitting in a chair.

"Feel a little better?"

155

Jorge still didn't know what to say. Who was this guy? He used to live in the apartment building one floor up, then he disappeared. Now, he'd come back, both last night and today. Jorge thought he'd killed him. What did he mean about a small miracle? Was it all a bad dream? "I . . . I . . . Yeah."

Elwin handed him the worn copy of John's gospel. "I think you left this at the women's shelter last night."

"How?"

Elwin's only answer was a wry smile. "Follow me. We'll find a quiet place to talk." They traversed the warren of halls. "Remember when Sanjay told you about God working on a supernatural level?"

"I think so."

"Remember the guards when you first went to the shelter looking for Carmen?"

"Can't forget those guys."

"Do you know who they were?"

He shook his head. "Some security force. I knew I couldn't go past them."

"You're right. You wouldn't have. Would you be surprised if I told you they were angels?"

Jorge's mouth opened. No sound came out. Finally he found his voice. "Angels?" he shook his head. "No."

"Yes, Jorge. Angels. Did you expect wings and halos? Now come, we'll sit in this little chapel here." Elwin led him into a windowless room. At the far end a soft light played across a plain table draped with a white linen cloth. On top lay a large open Bible flanked by two white candles in short polished brass candlesticks. An eight foot tall dark brown rough-hewn wood cross hung on the wall behind the table. Four short dark oak pews sat on either side of a center aisle. "Let's sit here." Elwin slid into the back pew on the right and moved over to give Jorge room.

Jorge studied Elwin for a moment. Why hadn't he died? Could he be an angel too? He didn't look like an

156

angel, but then, what did he expect? Those guards didn't look like angels either. "What's this with angels? Are you one too?"

"Let's just say I'm one of the Lord's servants, sent to do his bidding."

"So, what now?"

"Now, Jorge I want you to open the little booklet of John's gospel and turn to chapter three. While you read it, I'm going to leave. You probably won't see me again, but Pastor Andrew will be along and you can talk with him. Remember, there is nothing to fear with the Lord. God loves you, Jorge. He loves you more than you can imagine."

Jorge opened the little booklet and began to read. The words looked different this time as they drew him into the nighttime garden meeting. Engrossed in the scene, he didn't hear Elwin leave.

He looked up when Andrew sat beside him. "Ahh. . . That guy. I thought I knew him, but now, I'm not sure. Do you know him?"

Andrew shook his head. "He came here early this morning, and when we spoke he said you'd be coming here. He told me you'd need a shower, clean clothes, and a bed. When I asked him how he knew he began talking about a lady who used to work here. A large black woman. She was almost psychic." Andrew paused. "Funny how their names are so similar. He said he'd make sure you were situated and then he'd be gone. Something about an appointment."

"Do you think he could be an angel?"

"I do believe they sometimes help us, but. . . " Andrew shook his head. "And angel? Sort of a stretch, don't you think?"

Jorge shrugged.

"I see you have the little book with John's gospel. That's not the same one I gave you, is it?"

"Yeah, it is."

"I thought you left it, when you talked with Sanjay."

The scene flashed across his mind when he threw it in anger on the table and stormed out. "I did."

"Did you go back to get it?"

"No. Elwin gave it to me a few minutes ago. See. It's still got the places you marked for me." Jorge flipped to the back and the story of Peter. "He told me to read the story in chapter three again. Just like the little Indian guy did."

A knowing smile spread across Andrew's face as he put his arm around Jorge's shoulders. "I think maybe you're ready to believe now."

"I have many sins."

"The Lord can wash them all away, and give you a new heart."

"How can I do this?"

"Like Nicodemus. Believe in his gift, Jorge. Believe in his power, in his salvation. Just ask God for forgiveness, and to change your heart. Ask him to take your anger away. One thing I am sure of, God sent Elwin to bring you here."

"You know what he told me? He told me I needed a little miracle to bring me to my senses. He said he was a messenger of the Lord, but I think he must have been an angel."

"Maybe. Those things have happened before."

"Can you help me pray?"

"Of course."

Jorge dropped to his knees. Andrew knelt beside him, and wrapped his arm around Jorge's shoulder.

Chapter 36

Bob Johnston gulped down a couple of antacid tablets before he picked up the phone. After finding the number in his planner, he dialed. He needed to talk with his son, Neil. The boy was wasting his life and brains on nothing more than scum. As usual, his call went to voice mail. He waited for the beep. "Son, I'd like you to have lunch with me tomorrow. Let's meet at Breeze in the Century Plaza Hotel. I'll make reservations for twelve thirty. See you then." He took a breath and let it out slowly. "And wear your good jacket, okay."

Bob settled himself at the table and opened the menu. As a waiter passed by the aroma of grilled steak wafted through the air. His mouth began to salivate. He'd order the steak after his son arrived.

"Hello, Dad. I hope my attire meets with your approval."

Bob looked up and smiled. The suit was a cheap off the rack navy blue worsted, but passable. "You look fine. You didn't have to get a new suit, you know."

"Bought it for court a couple weeks ago. How are you, Dad?"

"Sit, Neil. Let's enjoy lunch. Have you tried the Rib Eye here?"

"No, Dad. You should know this isn't where I usually have lunch. In fact, most days I brown—"

"You could. Just shuck the idealistic notion you're helping people by working for the law center. It's a pathetic place. A waste of your talents. Go to work for one of the big firms. I sent you to Harvard to get a degree where you could make something of yourself."

Neil opened his menu and held it between them.

"I've got contacts, son. I can get you an interview."

Neil folded his menu and laid it across his plate. "We've had this conversation before. I like working there. I have a case now where this guy was wrongly sentenced under the three strikes law. He—"

"I don't believe it. You're trying to get a criminal out of prison so he can do it all over again. Did you read the article I e-mailed you on recidivism?"

"No. I don't believe I did. I've been a little busy trying to keep innocent people out of jail."

"Oh! That's a good one. How good are you at finding technicalities for these felons to skate on?"

Neil closed his eyes and shook his head.

Time to push a little harder. Neil needed to see the error of his ways. Needed to get rid of his liberal ideas. Needed to realize what life in the adult world was really like. "What's the matter, son? Did I hit a sore point?"

"I refuse to have this argument with you, Dad. I've made it plain in the past where I stand. I know what you believe. We're neither one going to change. Let's just agree we disagree." He picked up the menu. "What's good besides the Rib-eye?"

Bob sighed. The boy might never learn. He clenched his jaw and took a slow breath. He could pick up the battle another day. Now, he'd try to make this a pleasant meal. "You might try the Filet with Béarnaise

160

or the Sea Bass."

Neil shook his head. "A little too much for me. I think I'll have something lighter. I have to be in court at two-thirty."

"I guess you'll forego the wine too?"

Neil shrugged. "Sorry, Dad."

Bob tried to center himself. Avoid any further confrontation. "Don't worry about it. I should have allowed you more time to plan so we could spend the afternoon." He shook out his napkin and laid it on his lap. "By the way, I've been meaning to ask what did you do with all of grandmother's things? The stuff she left you in her will. Couldn't have been much value in the furniture from the dump she lived in."

"Why?"

"Curious is all."

"You took her bank accounts. Isn't that what you wanted?"

Bob gritted his teeth and glared at his son. "That, Neil, is impertinent."

"Sorry, Dad. Must be the sleazy lawyer in me poking it's ugly head out."

The waiter came and Bob ordered the Rib-eye and a bottle of '90 Opus. "Shame you couldn't join me, Neil. We could enjoy a pleasant afternoon."

Neil looked up at the waiter. "I'll have the Caesar salad."

"With the chicken or salmon, sir?"

"The grilled salmon, please. And just water to drink."

After the waiter left Bob said, "Since you refuse to talk about your misguided ideals, tell me about the furniture. You using it, or did you give it away?"

"Does it matter?"

"I suppose not. Although the dresser might have some value as an antique."

"It's always about the money, isn't it?"

"Is there anything else?"

"Dad, have you ever wondered why I chose to help people who need it? Why I'm using my law degree to make things a little better for people who can't afford it? Why I don't care about getting rich?"

Bob Johnston thought for a moment. "I always supposed it was because your grandmother put her religious clap-trap in your head as you grew up." A scowl marred his face. "I'm sorry I let her."

"You're sorry. I can't believe it. You didn't really know her. Your own mother. Grandma didn't put anything in my head. She was the kindest person I ever knew. She lived a cheerful, satisfied life. I saw her contentment and compared it to you. . . to your constant striving, your angst. I decided I'd rather be happy and content than greedy. Dad, I can see you, and you've put on a good façade, but down inside I expect you're miserable and empty." He paused a moment. "Sorry for the speech."

Bob clenched his fists and seethed inside, but somehow the kid had poked a hole in his philosophy of life.

The waiter brought their order, and Bob dove into his steak while Neil picked at his salad.

After they'd eaten in silence for awhile Bob said, "That's what you think?"

"What?"

"That I'm miserable?"

"Be honest with yourself. Aren't you?"

"I'm fine, son. I'm fine. You're the one who should be miserable, living in squalor among the degenerates in your flea-bag apartment."

Neil stood, his salad half eaten. "I need to head to court. Thanks for the lunch, Dad."

Bob Johnston picked at his steak, but somehow the meat's flavor turned to cardboard in his mouth. He wished he'd been able to connect with Neil. Everything he stood for told him the boy was bullheaded and misguided. He swirled the glass of Opus, smelled the fruit and hints of chocolate. He wondered, could it be the chasm between them wasn't so much about their differences? Could it be possible, Neil, despite his antagonistic manner, might have a point? He'd find out. He took a swallow of the Opus, then called the waiter for the check.

Chapter 37

Bob watched the afternoon courthouse crowd until it began to thin. The exchange in the restaurant, so out of character for his son, rankled at the time, and had troubled him daily ever since. He'd spent the past week in research to prepare for this afternoon. Today his son would argue a case. He wanted to see what really made the boy tick. Maybe he could glean some insight into what motivated him; why he spurned wealth and success.

He slipped into a seat in the back row as the judge took his place. The bench seats reminded him of the pews at church when his mother took him as a young boy. They smelled faintly of old varnish. The judge rapped his gavel lightly. As everyone settled in their places a slightly built man with a swarthy complexion and short-cropped salt and pepper curly hair slid into place beside him. He wore an expensive looking hand tailored silk suit, crisp white shirt with ruby cuff links, and muted two-tone wine colored tie. Burgundy Berluti loafers completed his wardrobe.

While the court clerk announced the first case the man leaned over and whispered, "You a witness?"

Bob studied the man and wondered. He wanted to tell him to mind his own business. He responded sotto voce, "Just watching."

"Me too, although I do know the man they're trying to get released. That's him." The slight man pointed out a tall, gaunt black man in an orange jail jumpsuit being led into the courtroom from a side door. He let himself down into his chair slowly at the defendant's table, as though in some discomfort.

Bob continued in a quiet voice so the people in the row ahead wouldn't be disturbed. "You know him?"

"We shared a cell at county for a few days."

This man's clothes didn't fit with knowing a convicted felon. Didn't fit with being in jail. Could he be a white collar criminal? He seemed more like a distinguished businessman from somewhere in the Mediterranean. Something didn't fit here. Bob's curiosity surged to the fore. The question slipped out before he could stop himself. "You were in jail?"

"Unfortunately, but it gave me the opportunity to meet Jahleel. It took some time, but I discovered he's a good man, and he shouldn't be in jail. Although I suppose at the time it served a purpose." He sucked in his lower lip as though in thought. "I hope his lawyer is able to persuade the judge to vacate his sentence. Let him out with time served."

Despite the man's wrong-headed point of view he seemed pleasant. He didn't seem dangerous even if he dabbled in white collar crime. "I'm sorry, I don't even know your name."

"Demos. I know it's different. From Greece. Don't ask how I got it. And my last name has too many k's and u's to pronounce."

"Glad to meet you. I'm Bob Johnston." He reached over and shook hands with the Greek. "The lawyer up there is my son. I don't know much about what he's doing. I thought he planned to be a corporate lawyer

165

for a big firm. He surprised me, doing this charity work. I'm not sure it's the right thing for him. This kind of experience on his resume could be a career breaker."

"If your son is working for this man's freedom, you should be proud of him."

Proud to have Neil get a criminal out of jail? This Demos fellow seemed as wrong-headed as his son. Bob edged away from Demos and crossed his legs.

Neil stood to speak to the judge. He argued with passion. He cited case law and precedent, validated by the State Supreme Court, to have what he called a miscarriage of justice reversed. He asked to have the sentence given to Jahleel under the three strikes law vacated. Bob listened to his son and thought if he could reason so effectively for someone who couldn't pay, the rewards from someone who could would be overwhelming. Why wouldn't he? Why did Neil shun success and wealth? If he wanted to be a do-gooder, he could volunteer his services on occasion. If the boy went to work for a good law firm, he could still do some pro-bono work. That's the argument he'd use the next time the two had a talk. He'd make sure to schedule it when Neil didn't have a pressing appointment. Give them time to have a serious talk.

The judge's gavel brought Bob back to the present. "This hearing is adjourned. I'll render my decision tomorrow morning at ten."

The next day Bob found Demos sitting in the back of the courtroom, a vacant place beside him. He acknowledged him with a brief smile as he sat next to him, careful to leave some space between them.

"Back to see if your son made sufficient points?"

"Something like that. I suppose you want to see if the guy you called a good man is freed?"

"Ah, yes. You guessed correctly." Demos gave Bob Johnston a studied look. "I don't think the man is well.

It would be good for him to have a little freedom."

They paused while the bailiff called the court to order and asked everyone to stand. He announced the judge, who then took his seat at the bench. Everyone sat.

Bob looked at Demos and whispered, "I suppose I shouldn't say this, but I read some statistics on recidivism. He'll probably go back to his life of crime."

"I wouldn't be too sure."

"Why?"

"I think I might have influenced him. He's had a change of heart. His focus now is on something quite the opposite than his life of crime."

The judge rapped his gavel.

"Looks like we're about to find out the ruling."

After a few brief remarks the judge looked directly at Williams. "It is the finding of this court that Mr. Jahleel Allen Williams' civil rights were violated. A clearly defined misdemeanor was incorrectly charged and prosecuted as a felony. I am therefore expunging his sentence under the three strikes law and amending his sentence for his last crime to be time served. Mr. Williams you are free to go. However. . ." The judge looked at Williams.

Neil stood. "Your honor, my client understands you don't want to hear of him coming before the bench again."

Jahleel's head bobbed assent.

The judge leaned forward. "You took the words from my mouth. See that it doesn't happen, Mr. Williams. We will take a brief recess before the next case. Court will reconvene in twenty minutes."

Neil and Jahleel stood and embraced.

Bob Johnston turned to tell Demos he got his wish, but the little Greek had disappeared. Instead of moving out of the courtroom Bob edged forward to try and hear the conversation between Neil and Jahleel.

The first words he overheard came from the freed criminal. "Thank you, Mr. Johnston. Thank you. I don't know how I can ever repay you."

Neil put his hand on Jahleel's shoulder and looked at him with a steady gaze. "Very simple, man. Like I told you before, like the judge said, don't get in trouble again. Next time—"

"Oh, I know. You don't got to worry none. I'll never go down that path again. I've been studying with pastor Andrew from the shelter. He comes by the jail every other day. I never thought I'd say this, but last week I gave my life to the Lord. What's left of it anyway. If Jesus gives me long enough to live, I'm gonna to be a preacher just like pastor Andrew."

Neil looked perplexed. Worry lines crept up between his eyes. "Did I hear you right? pastor Andrew?"

"Yep. Him and the Greek I shared a cell with. I fought it all the way, sort of like the poet, Francis Thompson. Glad God didn't give up on me either."

Bob Johnston had heard enough. These forces were more than he could understand. Something like his mother's crazy religious ideas, but he'd never paid much attention as a child. How? A criminal turned from crime by a preacher and the mysterious Greek businessman? Or could it be something else? Maybe a well-played façade. He turned and followed the rest of the people from the courtroom. He needed to find the Greek and this Andrew guy at some shelter. He needed answers.

Chapter 38

"You're a difficult man to find," Bob Johnston said as he settled into a straight-backed chair across a small table from Pastor Andrew. The hard wood poked his shoulders. He tried to find a more comfortable position.

"I don't try to be. What brings you here to Gateway?"

"In court two weeks ago I saw this black man. I can only assume he'd been a hardened criminal." He broke Andrew's gaze and looked at the floor. "Maybe he still is. One of those liberal judges freed him."

"And you've come here because?"

"It's a long story."

Andrew leaned back in his chair and smiled. "They almost always are. I have some time."

Bob tried to hide it, but a worried feeling crept into his voice. "I need to explain." He couldn't remember ever explaining anything to anyone, but he needed this one person to understand. He'd searched everywhere he could think of for the Greek without finding a trace of the man. If the religious nonsense was real, if he was going to understand Neil, he needed answers. The preacher must know something. He felt hesitant, like a scared kid in the principal's office. He couldn't lose this one last contact. "My son. . . my son and I. . . we haven't always seen eye to eye. A few weeks ago I thought I'd try to have a talk with him." He stopped and swallowed. How much should he tell this stranger who'd supposedly turned a criminal's life around? "It didn't go the way I'd planned."

"Go on."

Bob told him about the lunch, about going to court, about the mysterious Greek, and about what he overheard Jahleel say. When he mentioned Jahleel's name the preacher's face changed.

Andrew leaned forward. Big smile. "Ah. . . you met one of God's newest ambassadors."

"I don't know. That's what brings me here. I've been troubled by this person my son persuaded the court to set free. Is this criminal really changed? How did this Greek and you do it?"

"Before you surmise too much, Mr. Johnston, let me assure you I don't have any power to change people." Andrew rubbed his chin. "Have I seen people change? Sure. Hundreds of them. Do I think Jahleel is changed? Of course. Will it last forever?" He paused a moment. "Only time will tell."

"So he might return to a life of crime?"

"I doubt it, but it's always a possibility. God doesn't shackle people against their will."

"Oh, yes. I almost forgot you have to subscribe to the mumbo-jumbo of the God factor."

Andrew held Bob's gaze. "Mr. Johnston, I think the only way you'll believe is if you meet some people whose lives God has changed. I could try to persuade you for hours but. . ." He took a deep breath and sighed. "A little solid evidence sometimes helps. Right now, though, I don't think you believe any of this, mumbo-jumbo as you call it. So, do you have an hour or two to come with me? I'd like for you to talk with

Jahleel, and then a certain young woman. Let them tell their story."

"Well. . ."

"If you want to know how and why they changed you'll have to hear it from them."

Not the direction he wanted. Maybe the preacher knew where to find the Greek. "You remember the Greek fellow I told you about?"

"Of course."

"Do you know where I can find him?"

"No. I'm sorry. I truly don't. I think he travels a lot. Sometimes I see him. More often, I don't."

If he couldn't find the Greek. . . "So you think perhaps this Jahleel fellow can tell me something?"

"Come with me. You can ask him."

Seeing the criminal, Jahleel, seemed to be the only avenue left. He didn't like the idea, but what could he lose? Two hours the man said. He'd spent almost three weeks hunting for the Greek and this preacher. Bob nodded.

"I'll need to make a couple of phone calls to confirm we can see them both."

Bob rose.

Andrew motioned him to sit. "Stay. I don't mind you overhearing the calls." He flipped through his Rolodex, pulled out two cards, and dialed. When he'd hung up from the second call he said, "Everything's set. My car is parked around back."

They piled into Andrew's twelve-year-old musty smelling Plymouth mini-van and headed across the city. Thirty minutes later they parked in front of a dirty pink stucco building. Four mailboxes beside the front entrance told of the conversion from house to apartments. Gaping cracks scarred the front sidewalk and steps.

Andrew said, "Need to watch your step. Jahleel has a little efficiency apartment on the second floor."

171

Bob followed Andrew up the narrow, creaky stairs. The door opened almost immediately to Andrew's knock. The last time Bob saw Jahleel he wore a bright orange jail jumpsuit. His attire now, much less flamboyant, a pair of well used khaki pants and an old gray sweatshirt. The tiny apartment lacked pictures on the walls or other décor, but had a clean, scrubbed feel to it. The worn linoleum boasted a new coat of wax. The sparse collection of furniture consisted of a Formica topped table. Its worn surface told of better days in the distant past. Three mismatched chairs sat around it. A collection of prescription bottles and an open Bible were in front of one chair. A worn aqua Naugahyde sofa sat against one wall.

"Come in Pastor." He looked at Bob. "And I'm sorry, I don't know your name, but if you're with Pastor Andrew, you're welcome." He motioned the two in. "It's not much, but it's enough. Better than where I used to be."

Andrew shook Jahleel's hand. "Jahleel, this is Bob Johnston. He has some questions. I thought you might be able to help him with."

Jahleel shook Bob's hand in a limp grip. "Johnston. My lawyer's name was Johnston."

"I'm his father."

Jahleel took a step back. "Ohhhh." He drew the word out, and narrowed his eyes.

"Relax Mr. Williams. I only have some questions. I hope your answers may help me understand my son and give me a better idea of how you've changed your life," He shot the criminal a hard glare. "Like you say you have."

Jahleel pulled a chair from the table, and placed it near the sofa. "I guess you guys better sit down. Ask away."

"I sat in court the other day when my son argued your case. I—"

"So you know about some of the stuff I done?"

"Enough. After the judge gave his ruling I walked forward and overheard a little of what you said to Neil. It took some hunting before I found the pastor here. I'm afraid there's no way to say this gently. I have some doubts about your changed life."

Jahleel closed his eyes and sighed. "Mr. Johnston, I never thought I'd change either, but God just wouldn't let me go. I'm not proud of what I done through my life, and I gots me some kind of heart condition. I thought I'd probably die in stir. The person who started bugging me about Jesus. . . " A grin appeared. "This weird little dude when I was in county lock-up. Man, I was mean to him. I did everything but stomp the guy. But he just wouldn't quit."

"A Greek with an unusual name?"

Jahleel chuckled. "Gotta be him."

"He sat beside me in court."

"Demos." A broad smile filled Jahleel's face. His eyes sparkled. "I wish I'd known he came to court. I woulda thanked him. Do you know where he is?"

"No. I only met him in the courtroom. But you say this man, Demos, and the preacher here, changed you?"

"No sir. They just pointed the way. Them and a girl I knew once. She prayed for me. Demos and Pastor Andrew they hounded me. They never quit. But they didn't change me. No sir." He closed his eyes and rocked back and forth for a moment. "Jesus. He changed me. Filled me with his love. Took away my sins by dying for me. I don't suppose you'd understand, but I'm studying now to be a preacher. I hope I have enough time left on this earth to do some good. Point someone to the Lord."

Bob stared at Jahleel. What could he say? What could he ask?.

Jahleel paused a moment. "I mighta been locked in prison before and the judge let me out, but Jesus freed me from somethin' way worse than prison. He set me free from my sins. Set me free from thinking sex and drugs were the best life could give me. Changed my heart, he did. He gave me peace and compassion, right here. Yessiree." Jahleel pointed to his chest with a thin finger.

Bob Johnston wondered. Could this be a well-practiced façade? A simple frightened criminal turning to religion because of some illness? Maybe the man had changed, but why, and was it real? He didn't know what to say. He rose and started for the door then turned toward Jahleel. "I can't say you've answered my questions, but thank you for your time."

Who did the preacher want him to see next? Some girl? It probably wouldn't explain any more, or answer any questions. Just spout more nonsense like Neil believed. Like his mother tried to cram into him when he was a kid. When they were in the car, he'd tell the preacher to take him back to the shelter.

Chapter 39

As Andrew's ancient Plymouth chugged across the city, Bob studied the preacher. "Much as I appreciate your efforts, I don't think talking to anyone else is going to help answer my questions. This Jahleel fellow might think he's turned his life around, but my time spent listening to him was a waste."

Pastor Andrew made a U-turn at the next intersection. "As you wish, Mr. Johnston. I can't force you, but I think your time would be well-spent to listen to one more person's experience. It might answer your questions. In any case I think you'll find it interesting."

"This is the woman you called?"

Pastor Andrew focused on the road ahead. "Uh-huh."

Bob already had his fill of redemption from drugs and finding Jesus. "So she has nothing to do with Jahleel?"

"Quite the contrary, Mr. Johnston. Remember, he said three people influenced his decision to follow Jesus. This woman is the girl he mentioned."

"Why didn't you tell him we were going to see

her?"

"When you hear her story you'll understand."

Could the two of them be enemies? At odds with each other like he and Neil? His curiosity rose. "All right. I'll go."

Pastor Andrew did another U-turn.

The apartment building they parked near looked considerably better than Jahleel's. Trimmed bushes flanked a short walkway to the entrance and bordered a postage-stamp lawn. Three doors led from a tiny vestibule. Andrew pushed the buzzer for Number Two. A middle-aged Hispanic lady answered.

Andrew said, "Hello Carmen. I—"

"Buenos días, Pastor Andrew. Tiff's in her bedroom freshening up. She should be right out. Is this the man you talked to her about?"

He nodded. "Mr. Johnston, I'd like you to meet Tiffany's roommate, Carmen Ramirez."

Carmen shook Bob's hand. "Glad to meet you. Please come in and have a seat." She ushered them into a small living room, and settled them on the sofa. Three candles glowed on a side table and gave off the faint aroma of lilacs. "Can I get you something to drink? Iced tea? Water?"

Andrew said, "Perhaps some iced tea if it's not any trouble. No sugar for me."

"Same here." Bob watched Carmen disappear into the kitchen and heard the clinking of glasses. Before she returned, a young blonde appeared wearing loose jeans and a white blouse with little appliqués on the front. Her still damp flaxen hair hung halfway down her back. She wore a pale lip-gloss and a bit of blush on her cheeks. To Bob, she looked like the stereotypical scrubbed, girl-next-door. What connection did she have to Jahleel? Why would a young girl like this pray for a criminal? Then he began to appraise her more carefully. Different clothes. Make-up to enhance her features. The figure she'd carefully downplayed. She could pass for a model. Hmmm. I wonder.

"Hi, Pastor Andrew. Sorry I wasn't ready when you came. I've spent the whole day in my sweats studying. Big Sociology test tomorrow. Time got away from me." She leaned down and gave him a hug then tucked her hair behind an ear when she straightened.

As Andrew introduced Bob to Tiffany, Carmen returned with three glasses of iced tea. "I'm going to go. Give you three some privacy."

Tiffany sat in a nearby chair and smiled at Carmen. "You know all about me Carmen. I don't have any secrets."

"I know, but it'll be easier this way. Besides I have to get ready for my shift at the hospital pretty soon."

After Carmen left Pastor Andrew said, "Tiffany, before you tell Mr. Johnston your story I think I should give you a little background of why we're here." He looked at Bob with raised brows.

"Sure. Fine."

"Mr. Johnston witnessed a court hearing a couple of weeks ago, and came to see me with questions. His son was the attorney arguing a case and he represented—"

"Say no more, Pastor." Her face sobered. "Jahleel, right?"

"You're as bright and perceptive as ever."

Tiffany turned away. "I know I don't have to be afraid any longer, not since I gave my life to Jesus, but with our history. . . I guess it'll take some time for all the anxiety to go away." She brightened. "I am glad he's out of jail and he's found the Lord. Is it true he's going to study to be a minister?"

"Already enrolled at a Bible college. I'm sure God has a work for him. When we talked he credited you with helping him find his way to Christ."

"You're kidding? How?" Her eyes grew wide. "I didn't do anything."

Andrew smiled. "Sometimes it's the littlest thing. The other day he told me about the letter you wrote him while he was in prison. He's saved it all this time. He keeps it in his Bible at Luke, chapter ten. Says you were his first Good Samaritan. Your letter began his journey to Jesus."

"Does he know the rest?"

"I'm not sure, but count on it, someday he'll figure it out."

Bob listened, puzzled at the conversation. Questions piled up in a line, waiting to be answered. What had this young woman done? How did she know Jahleel? Why weren't the two of them in contact now?

"I'm sorry," Tiffany said as she turned to Bob. "You came to hear my story, and I'm sure with our rattling on you have a few questions too."

Bob sat open mouthed and nodded.

"I've known Jahleel for some time, and my past isn't any prettier than his. You know he was involved in drug dealing and prostitution?"

"The drugs, yes, but not. . . " The realization of the life she hinted at stunned Bob. "You?" He eyed her differently.

"I'm afraid so. Not a pretty part of my life. Jahleel called me his favorite girl. I did five, six tricks a night for him. He used the money to buy heroin, and then resold some. He hooked me on the drugs too. I knew the smack would kill me sooner or later, so one night when I needed a fix really bad I went to Wayfarer's. I wanted to kick the drugs. I wanted to save my life. After I got inside, even though I knew it was the right place to be, I tried to leave. A lady named Elwina worked there. She wouldn't let me go. She loved me like a daughter all the way through withdrawal. She told me it wasn't her, it was really Jesus' love. Elwina was like an angel."

"What about the letter you wrote?"

"Oh, that. I found out about Jahleel's illness. Something with his heart. So I made a few phone calls and between Pastor Andrew and me we got the prison doctor to send him for tests. He's on medicine now, so he should be fine. And he's found Jesus, just like I did."

"But you don't want to see him, even though you helped him?"

"Seeing each other wouldn't be good for either of us. There's a lot of unpleasant memories." She shook her head. "Least for me."

"So you hate him?"

"Oh, no, Mr. Johnston. I forgave him long ago, but. . . but I gotta move on." She straightened. "I believe in looking at the future, not the past."

Bob wondered if his history with Neil was so insurmountable it would keep them apart. "But you're glad about what's happened to him?"

"Of course. You don't know how hard I prayed for him."

Amazing. This young woman who used to be a hooker, now going to college, and her pimp studying to be a preacher. It didn't make sense. How could it be real? Neil, satisfied with a simple apartment and working for people who couldn't afford legal help, poked a hole in his belief. A part of him longed to have the kind of happiness these people seemed to possess.

Pastor Andrew interrupted his thoughts. "Do you have any questions for Tiffany?"

"Uh. . . I guess not." What would he say? "Besides I should get back to my office. I still have a lot to do today."

"All right, then." Andrew turned to Tiffany. "Thanks for your time Tiff."

As they left, Bob made note of the address.

In the car when Andrew asked him what he thought Bob said, "Two interesting people. I need time to think about what they said, so don't give me a sales pitch. Okay?" They'd obviously convinced themselves they'd found something. Then, again, an attractive girl like Tiffany. . . with her history and looks, maybe she'd gone out on her own. It wouldn't hurt to find out. He'd go see her some evening when the roommate had gone to work.

"No problem. When you have more questions, give me a call."

They drove the rest of the way back to the shelter in silence.

Chapter 40

A pair of men crouched against the wall in an alley not far from the women's shelter.

"Well, Alderon," said the taller of the two, "What did you observe as you followed Bob Johnston on this little journey? Did you discover anything that might give us an opening? Something to further his drift away from the enemy and into the darkness?"

"Yes, Master. When he left Tiffany's he glanced at the address. I think he intends to return. I'm certain he doesn't want to learn more of the enemy's lies." Alderon couldn't help but chuckle. "He does have this penchant for sex. He gave Tiffany more than one appraising glance during his visit to her home with the preacher."

"So if he returns?"

"Not if, Heylel, when." A grin split Alderon's face. "I think we might not only assure Bob Johnston's continued glide toward hell, but drag Tiffany back too. She's struggling financially while she goes to college. A little whoring for the money would be an easy slide away from the enemy. . . and then back to the drugs again." He couldn't hold back a long laugh of satisfaction.

"Your mind is truly devious, Alderon. You should be proud. Now, off with you. There's work to do."

Chapter 41

Eleven days later Bob drove back to the Wayfarer's shelter. In the interim he'd returned to Tiffany's apartment. He'd offered her an ocean view condo in Santa Monica. Freedom to come and go as she pleased. He couldn't believe it when she'd rebuffed him. It seemed she really had changed. He found it impossible to understand her mind-set, her devotion to her new belief.

His work suffered from the turmoil in his mind. He needed to ask the preacher one more question. As soon as he stepped from his car and locked the doors with a chirp of the electronics he knew he should have called first. He looked at the sun, a giant orange globe, dipping behind the city skyline in the west. What if the preacher wasn't there? What if he'd gone home, or wherever he went at night? When he strode in the entrance a large woman, dressed in a bright red and yellow Caftan, met him.

"Welcome to Wayfarer's, sir." She smiled a four hundred watt smile as she reached to shake his hand. "How can I help you?"

Bob could hear his heart beating, hammering in his

chest. "I'm looking for Pastor Andrew." He pulled his hand from hers quickly. Her hand felt warm, too warm, but more than that. Her touch sent a tingle of electricity through him. "I. . . I hope he's in."

"I'm so sorry. The pastor's visiting someone in jail. I don't know when he'll be back." A long pause. "Maybe tomorrow."

Deflated, Bob turned to leave.

"You wouldn't be Mr. Johnston would you, now?" The woman's words hauled him back.

How did she know? Did Pastor Andrew say something to her?

"Ahhh, yes."

"I's been expecting you. My name's Elwina."

The name sounded familiar. He'd never met this woman, but he'd heard the name before. Somewhere, then it came to him. The girl, Tiffany. "You. . . you used to work here? How did you know my name?"

"Let's just say God has his ways. Sometimes we don't understand. You're troubled and you've come with a question for Andrew. Let's see if I can help." She motioned for him to follow her.

"You're just going to leave the entrance open?"

She laughed. "Don't worry none. It'll be all right. Now come." She led the way down a hall to a small chapel, and sat in the back pew.

Bob Johnston didn't know what to do. What powers did this woman have? He could leave and come back tomorrow, but the need to have an answer had been growing in him like a child struggling to be born. If he didn't find out it threatened to tear him apart. He must have the issue settled. He sat slowly beside the woman, careful to leave some space between them. He didn't want another jolt of electricity.

"You want to know. . ." she said with measured words, as she locked him in her gaze. "You want to know what you have to give up to possess the peace

184

and joy Tiffany and Jahleel have, and yes, your son Neil, too."

Her words stunned him. She not only knew he came wanting an answer, but the question, too. How did she know him? How did she know his mind? He could believe she might know Tiffany and Jahleel, but she even knew about Neil. There was something crazy going on here. Something he couldn't comprehend.

Elwina broke into a broad smile. "You look surprised, Mr Johnston. You shouldn't be. I told you God works in mysterious ways. Not always this direct, but he does work. Now tell me, how close did I get to your question?"

Bob still hadn't found his voice. He stared at her.

"Pretty much on the mark, I 'spect."

He nodded.

"You're guessing God'll ask you to give up the wealth you've worked your whole life to get, aren't you? And I 'spect there's a bit more. You don't want to give up what you'd call fun." The woman's dark eyes burned into him. "Shocked you too, when Tiffany turned down your offer, and told you to go. But mostly it's about gettin' the money, and hanging onto it."

He felt his heart thumping in his chest. This woman knew everything. His breath came in jagged gasps. He feared he would have a heart attack.

"Don't worry none, now. You're goin' to be just fine." She chuckled. "Your heart won't pop over what I said. Do you know how many rich people there are who love God and serve him?"

He tried to calm himself with deep breaths. "I. . . I wouldn't think there would be any." His mind flashed to something he'd heard in church as a kid. "Doesn't the Bible say something about a camel going through the eye of a needle?"

"God isn't against wealth, Mr. Johnston." Elwina reached in the book rack on the back of the pew and drew out a Bible. She patted its cover. "In here are stories of dozens of rich people who loved God. There's Job, and Abraham, and Solomon, and Nicodemus, and Joseph of Arimathéa, to name a few. Those people weren't perfect, but they did love God. It's not the wealth, Mr. Johnston, it's letting money come between you and the Lord. When you make an idol of it, it can crowd him from your life. Just like the other things you want to hang onto. Some people can handle wealth, others can't. If you want to have his peace and love in your life, you'll have to decide where you are." She didn't speak for a long while. "Does what I've said make sense?"

"I. . . I guess so." He stopped and gazed for a moment at the cross on the front wall of the chapel. "I think my son knows himself better than I thought, and he's decided he can't chase riches."

"Now, the big question is, what do you want to do about your life? It's really quite simple. Do you want to experience the joy of Jesus?"

"I. . . I don't know." He took three deep breaths trying to calm himself. "Right now, I. . . " He stared at the floor. "I don't think I can."

"I'm sorry," she said.

He looked up to say something more to her, but she was gone. She'd disappeared. Vanished as though she'd never existed. Bob stood and wandered out into the street, alone in a cold late afternoon wind. He pulled his coat tightly around his body, and walked toward his car head down.

He could have sworn he heard an old man laughing long and loud. The sound came from around the corner in the alley. He went to see, but couldn't find anyone. An empty alley. The place smelled of garbage and urine. Graffiti adorned the walls. Mostly gang tagging. He turned to go, then looked again at the wall. Far down on the next building someone had spray-painted a six foot high bright red, upside-down star inside a circle. A frigid wind whipped down the alley and tore at his coat. When he reached his car he heard the laughter again.

Chapter 42

The wind howled across the mountain peaks and whipped through the barren crags. As before, Paragon kept a human form for this meeting. On the climb up the dusty trail he'd sensed, but never saw, someone following him. It must be the enemy. Who else would trail after him in this weather? He tried to push the thought from his mind, but it kept niggling at the edges of his consciousness. When he could see the summit, he sat cross-legged on the hard ground in the lee of a rock, his head bowed, while he waited for Sophio. The gusts irritated his eyes and made them water.

"You look dejected, friend."

Paragon raised his head at the sound of an unfamiliar voice and wiped away a tear with the back of his hand. "Aegus. It's good to see you, but I expected Sophio."

"I'm afraid Sophio's still occupied over in the Mideast war-zone. There's so much for him to do, but he's been sent help."

Paragon nodded, then pushed away a lingering drift of snow and motioned Aegus to sit.

"Your work has gone well, despite the recent

disappointment with Bob Johnston. Sometimes people don't heed the call to let Michael into their life and change their heart." Aegus sighed. "And of course you know the enemy must be rejoicing."

"I know. Still. . . " He let the thought die in the raging wind. He wondered, too, how many of the others he'd worked with would let their decision waver, would let their fledging faith be blown away like the leaves of autumn. What would happen with Sanjay, and Carmen, and Miguel, and the others.

"I'm sure you feel very much like Michael felt when he walked here two millennia ago. He felt the joy of seeing many let love into their hearts, but he also had disappointments. Remember?"

A knowing smile creased Paragon's face. "Oh, yes. Impossible to forget. The joy when we both sang with the others and announced his birth to the shepherds, the sorrow when some, like the rich ruler, turned away." A frown played across his features. "And there was Judas who turned away for thirty silver coins. The despair we felt when our lord hung on the cross, the thrill for all of us when he rose from the tomb. Now there's a great memory." He closed his eyes for a moment, then looked at Aegus. "And more good memories, than bad."

"Ah, yes. And soon the battle with the prince of darkness will be over."

Paragon reached across the space between them and gripped Aegus' arm. "Tell me, Aegus, am I being summoned back? It's taken a few months of time here, and I've made the needed interventions in all seven lives."

Aegus nodded. "Not yet, I'm afraid. As I said, you've done well, but there's a little more left to do."

He immediately became more alert. "What? Tell me."

"Someone else will be here soon to tell you. I have to go now."

"Who?"

Aegus shook his head as he began to glow, then vanished.

Paragon knew it wouldn't be long. He waited in the howling wind, not moving a muscle. Time seemed to drag. Funny, he thought, how acclimated he'd become to all the habits and behaviors here. He even felt a hint of irritation at the time it took. He closed his eyes and leaned back against the rock, until he sensed a presence. Then the wind stopped.

"There's no time for a nap, Paragon."

He opened his eyes. Impossible. Michael's special messenger. Whatever he had to do, it must be important. "Gabriel! This is a surprise."

Gabriel settled on the ground in front of Paragon. "There is one more task. Really any of us could, but since you are so familiar with these people already Michael thought it best to have you continue."

"Yes. Yes. Whatever Michael wants."

"It's Tiffany and Jahleel."

"And my mission?"

"You are to watch over Tiffany. Keep her safe. She can do much for Michael's cause. Already she is a great influence."

"Agreed, and Jahleel?"

"Jahleel needs to stay healthy. His heart condition is troubling. The medication will only help so long. He'll soon need to be put on a list for a transplant. He has an important message to carry to those who would listen only to him. He has the potential to persuade thousands, as Paul did two millennia ago. You'll need to influence doctors and others. Jahleel is a channel to complete a vital work for Michael. Keep him alive. And I'm sure I don't need to tell you Heylel and his minions will try their utmost to stop you. To keep you from completing your task." Gabriel reached out and put a hand on Paragon's shoulder. "Will you carry out this mission?"

"I'd count it a privilege to do this for Michael. He told you himself he wants me to do this?"

"He did. Now, like Aegus, I too must return." Gabriel became a blinding light, then vanished.

Paragon ran down the mountain until he began to smell the pungent aroma of pine needles and wood. His pace slowed when he found a road, and finally arrived at a tiny mountain village. Tomorrow he'd begin his new task. Could he succeed?

Chapter 43

Demos knocked lightly on the door to Jahleel's apartment and moved back a pace.

No answer.

He knocked again. Harder.

A lady in a thin cotton housecoat, and wearing fuzzy rabbit slippers, opened a door on the other side of the hall. She took the cigarette out of her mouth, blew smoke at him, and scowled. "Keep it down, will ya?"

"Sorry." When she closed the door Demos knocked again. Softer this time. This visit would be crucial. Could he, as Demos, influence Jahleel to stay courageous while he struggled with discouragement because of his HCM? How could the doctor cure him? Michael hadn't promised a healing miracle. How could he fulfill his mission?

A sleep laden voice came from the other side. "Yo. Who's there?"

"An old acquaintance."

"Don't know no old acquaintance. Go away."

"Hey, man. It's late. You've missed your first

class."

"Who are you?"

"I told you, Jahleel. Now, open the door. I need to see you." The dull roar of a jet from Burbank Airport vibrated the building.

"Hey, whoever you are. I don't deal no more. I'm tired, let me go back to sleep."

Demos shook his head. "I'm not here for drugs. I need to talk to you." He raised his voice even though it might cause the lady across the hall to yell again. "I'm not leaving 'til you open the door."

Noises filtered through the thin wood. "A sec. Okay?"

Demos waited.

Jahleel opened the door on a security chain. When he saw Demos through the opening he said, "Whoa. It's you. Never expected to see you again."

Demos grinned. "Come on, man. It can't be that big of a surprise."

Jahleel took the chain off and opened the door. He wore grey sweatpants, a sleeveless black knit shirt, and a pair of old maroon felt slippers. "How. . . how'd you find me?"

"School registrar. Not too hard. Can I come in?"

"Yeah, man. Gimmie a sec, Okay?" Jahleel stepped back from the door, picked up a pair of jeans and a plaid shirt from the back of a chair. "Yeah. Come on in." He disappeared slowly into the bedroom.

Demos stepped inside and waited.

Jahleel emerged still in the slippers, but dressed in the jeans and shirt. He pulled a chair from its place at the kitchen table and said, "Sit, man. Tell me, why'd you come see me?"

Demos watched Jahleel slowly lower himself into the other kitchen chair. "You look tired, friend."

"Beat, man. I see the doc once a month, but the

medicine ain't doing it's magic like it did at first. Got me on new pills too. Still I gotta take a day in the middle of the week to rest."

Demos leaned forward. "You're still going to school?"

"Yeah, man. I just don't know how much longer." A sigh escaped. "Maybe God don't want me to be a preacher."

"I think he does, Jahleel. Anyone who fought the Lord like you did will be a powerful witness. You have an innate ability to connect with people. You proved that before." Demos cracked a wry grin. "You proved it when your life centered on drugs and women. Now, with Jesus in your life, you can be as persuasive for Christ as Paul was."

"I don't have the energy, man." He shook his head. "I don't see how. . ."

"Has your heart doctor talked to you about anything else they can do?"

"Long time ago he mentioned a transplant, but you know how long you gotta wait on those lists. I'm gettin' down, man. . ." He took a labored breath. "Thinkin' maybe God wants me to live for him long as I can, then let it go."

"Did the doctor put you on a list?"

"I dunno. If he did. It don't matter none."

"It matters, Jahleel. It does."

Jahleel shrugged. "So you say."

"Tell me, what do you do when you get down?"

"Read Psalms, and then John. I pray too. Pray a lot."

"That's good," Demos said. "I don't want to tire you. I'll go now. Next time you see your doctor, make sure he's put you on a transplant list. I know it takes a long time. You never know. If it's supposed to happen, God'll find a way. Promise you'll talk to your doctor?"

"Yeah, man. I'll do it. You'll come back and see

me?"

"I will. Count on it. I can see myself out." Demos rose, bent down and embraced Jahleel. As he left the building he wondered if Jahleel meant what he'd promised. Had he been forceful enough with him? Would Jahleel live until the doctors could find him a new heart?

Chapter 44

The beige walls of Doctor Pang's examination room closed in on Jahleel. He couldn't catch his breath. Why was the doctor so late? He'd been sitting on the end of the examination table for over fifteen minutes. He tried to concentrate on his breathing. Maybe that would make the time go faster.

He heard the latch click before he saw the door open. Doctor Pang stepped into the room. The round faced physician greeted him, then sat on a stool in front of a built-in desk. He opened a chart, flipped on the computer monitor, and scanned the information before him. He hummed as he ran a finger across an EKG print-out, then turned to face his patient. "Well, Jahleel, tell me how you're feeling. Have you noticed a difference with the new medication?"

It took Jahleel a couple of breaths before he could respond. He shook his head. "Bad as ever, Doc."

Doctor Pang inhaled and let it out slowly all the while focused on Jahleel. He sucked in his lower lip, chewed on it a bit before he spoke. "The tests tell me the same thing. I've never seen anyone with HCM deteriorate as quickly as you have." He reached over and put a hand on Jahleel's shoulder. "I hoped this new drug would give us a little more time. I don't want to scare you, although I'm running out of options for your treatment."

"How long do I have, Doc?"

"We're not there yet, Jahleel. We've got a while. How often are you using the oxygen at home?"

"Most all the time."

"How about at night?"

"Nah, just daytime."

"But you didn't bring your portable tank with you when you came today?"

"Hate dragging the thing around. 'Sides it makes me look like I'm an invalid. Hate that too."

"I understand. However you better do it from now on. No. Make that, you must use oxygen all the time. We'll keep you on the meds you're taking. They've slowed the disease, but not as much as I'd hoped." Doctor Pang turned back to Jahleel's chart.

Silence hung in the room. His promise to Demos roared in his mind like an angry tornado. Getting on the transplant list would mean he was about finished. If he lasted long enough to get to the top of the list, they'd crack him open like a cooked lobster, and stick some stranger's heart in his chest. Maybe the operation wouldn't work any better than the medicine. A shiver shook him. He wanted to leave and go home and take a nap. But he'd made the promise to Demos. The little Greek never would let go. He'd dragged him kicking and screaming to the foot of the cross. Jahleel knew in his heart the little guy had been behind all the maneuverings to get him out of stir. He owed his freedom to Demos. He'd made him a promise.

"Ahh. . . Doc?"

Doctor Pang looked up from the chart. "Yes?"

"I know I'm in bad shape." Jahleel leaned forward. "I was wondering about. . . well, you mentioned once about a heart transplant."

"Hmmm. A transplant? It's a possibility, although I need to be frank with you. I'm afraid what I have to say isn't good news. Your blood type is A-B negative."

"What's that mean?"

"Your blood type is rare, Jahleel. Less than one percent of the population. It will take a donor with your blood type to be a match. Plus there are around fifty different antigens to consider." Doctor Pang twisted up his mouth and shook his head. "I'm afraid finding the right heart would be a long shot."

"So where does that leave me? Sounds like the short end of the stick."

"Not that bad." A grin creased Dr. Pang's face. "Confession time, Jahleel. I put you on the list some time ago, hoping the right donor heart would come along. I'd have been derelict in my duty if I hadn't. I knew it would take time. I haven't told you because I didn't want to get your hopes up, or have you believe everything was solved." He stroked his chin. "I'm afraid it still could be a long time to find the right donor. I hoped this new medication would be more effective."

Not as bad as he expected. "Uh, okay, Doc."

"I don't want to sound like a broken record, but your best bet now is to keep using your oxygen. Give your heart as much rest as you can. It's straining itself just to keep you alive. I want to see you again in a week." He fixed Jahleel with a steady look. "And bring your portable tank with you."

Jahleel scowled.

"I know. I know. You don't want to look like an invalid."

"Yeah, Doc. And I'll be alive. . . " Jahleel tried a half-hearted chuckle. "I guess that's better than the alternative."

"Next week?"

"I'll be here." Jahleel clenched his jaw and shook his head. "With my infernal tank."

Chapter 45

Tiffany raised her head from a book on Adolescent Psychology. Did she hear a noise? It couldn't be her roommate, Carmen, probably still asleep after a twelve-hour night shift at the hospital. She heard it again. A soft thump, thump, thump coming from the front door of their apartment. She marked her place and put the book aside.

Tiffany cracked the door open on its security chain. Shocked at the sight– Elwina. The same bright Caftan, the same wide smile, the same sparkling eyes with laugh lines at the corners. "Just a sec." She removed the security chain. "This is a surprise." She gave the woman a hug, felt Elwina's arms encircle her with affection. Tiffany felt so secure wrapped in the arms of this ample black woman. Elwina's hugs always brought back memories of their first meeting. The refuge she felt in the warmth of love. "Come in. Come in. I didn't know you were in town."

"Just happened to be in the neighborhood. I wanted to stop and give you a hug."

Tiffany ushered Elwina into the modest living room. "Now, Elwina, I know you're never just in the neighborhood." Tiffany rolled her eyes. "I gotta know why you came by. So, sit down and tell me."

Elwina shook her head as she settled her bulk on the sofa, and patted the place beside her. "You're too bright, girl. Just give me a moment or two. I'll get to things."

Tiffany sat beside her, then bounced up. "I'm forgetting my manners. Can I get you a drink? I think I have some sweet tea in the fridge."

"My, my. You do? I'd love some."

"Won't take me but a sec."

When Tiffany returned Elwina said, "Can't fool you, can I? You're too smart. I did come here, like you said, to bring you some news."

"Are you coming back to stay?"

"No. No. It's not news about me." Elwina took a large swallow of the tea. "My, my. This is so good. You sure you never lived down south? Your mama teach you how to make sweet tea when you were a little girl?"

"I'll bet you've figured me out better than that, Elwina. Never lived in the south and my mother didn't teach me nothin'." She paused. Should she go on? A deep breath before she continued. "Guess I didn't have much of a mother, an' no daddy either. My step-dad started visiting my bedroom when I turned twelve, so I ran away. Lived on the streets with a gang of kids for a couple years. Jahleel found me when I turned fourteen. The rest you know."

Elwina nodded.

Tiffany said, "Now, about the tea. I learned to make sweet tea from Cassie when I lived at the shelter." Tiffany smiled. "I think you taught her."

Elwina chuckled. "Guess I did. Guess I did." She patted Tiffany's hand and gave it a squeeze. "You know I never pried into your past. I wondered how long it'd take you to open up about it. I'm glad you did. Letting out those secrets is almost always liberating. But I'm more glad you came to the shelter and found Jesus."

"I'm glad too." She leaned over and gave Elwina a hug. "I still remember you blocking my way when I got scared and wanted to go back out on the street."

"Big question, girl. Been preyin' on my mind."

Tiffany tilted her head to the side, her eyes wide. "What?"

"I could ask how you doin'. I know you'll say you're fine." Elwina fixed her in a steady gaze. "You experienced some awful things growin' up. You oughta be a bit wary around men. How you doin' with those kind of relationships?"

"Okay, I guess."

"See. Just like I said. You'll say okay, or fine." Elwina shook her head. "You gonna be a social worker, girl. You gotta care about men just like women. Love 'em all."

"I know." She took a deep breath and let it out slowly before she continued. "I've been talking with a psychologist at the college about my hang-ups, and I talk to Sanjay every couple of weeks, too. They've both been a lot of help. I'm not angry anymore." A quick flash of memory made her tense. "Sometimes fear creeps in. There was this guy the other day, but I told him I didn't do that no more." She let out a breath she didn't realize she'd been holding in. "And I know all men aren't alike. There's Pastor Andrew, and Gordie, and Sanjay." She closed her eyes a moment. "And there's one other guy, too. Back when I. . . when I was a hooker." She stopped and took another breath. "He lived in the apartment building where Jahleel and I lived." She saw Elwina nod and smile. "Mr. Hunter." She felt a warm glow as she remembered. "He was the nicest man. Cared about everyone. . . like you do. I know he worried about me. I can't put my finger exactly on any specific thing he did or said, but because of him I decided I had to kick the drugs and

202

live. I know it's not possible, but I'd like to see him and tell him thanks for caring about me."

Elwina smiled. "See. You're learnin'. They's not all bad."

"Yeah. I guess you're right."

"Come on, now. You knows I'm right. And the bad ones can change, too."

Tiffany didn't know what to say. Silence hung in the air. She knew it. No doubt. Elwina was talking about Jahleel. She'd heard bits of information from Pastor Andrew, and Sanjay. And from Carmen too, who'd seen Jahleel once at the hospital.

"You did hear me, didn't you? And you knows who I'm talkin' about don't you?" Elwina patted her hand.

"Yeah. You have news about Jahleel?"

"I do." Elwina fixed Tiffany with a steady gaze. "I know he hurt you. . . bad. Makin' you sell your body, hookin' you on heroin. Tell me, have you forgiven him? Back then he was truly a bad person. I'd think it'd be hard to forgive him. So. . . have you?"

"A long time ago, Elwina. You know, if Jesus could forgive the soldiers who crucified him, and forgive me with all the stuff I've done. I have the Lord's love in my life. I couldn't do anything else but forgive him."

"Good. Shows your heart's full of Jesus' love. A heart chock-full of love means no room for hate, or hurt, or anger."

"I know. And it feels good."

"Now, Tiffany, I suppose you figgered I been busy scootin' around, stickin' my nose where it sometimes don't belong. Tryin' to find out as much as I could about Jahleel. You know I had a hand in gettin' him sent off to jail so he couldn't bother you back then, but this lawyer kid got him out. And he's given his life to the Lord now. Wants to be a preacher."

"Yeah. I heard."

"And I guess you know about his heart?"

Tiffany nodded.

"Well, it's not gettin' better. In fact, from what I can find out he's pretty bad off."

"Oh. I thought the doctors gave him medicine to make him well."

"It did for a while, but now it's getting' worse. He needs our prayers again, girlfriend." Elwina held Tiffany's hand. Gave it a squeeze. "Think you can pray for him?"

So much history with Jahleel. Not much of it good. Three-and-a-half-years of drugs and sex and torment. It almost killed her. She didn't want to see Jahleel, but she could pray. "I can do that. Yeah, I'll pray for him."

"There's one more thing."

"Ahh. . ." She wondered what Elwina would ask next.

"I think you need to write him a letter. Tell him you've forgiven him. Forgiveness is a wonderful medicine. Does way more to heal than any prescription. Do him good to hear you've forgiven him."

Tiffany remembered how she felt when she realized Jesus had forgiven her sins. Lightness and joy filled her life then. Elwina had asked. She couldn't refuse. But what would she say? What words should she use? With Jahleel out of prison, would he try to see her if she wrote? She wasn't ready to face him. Not yet. "It'll take me a while. And then I need his address."

"Don't worry 'bout no address. I'll come back by in a few days and pick your letter up. I can see he gets it."

/;

Chapter 46

The sound of a soft knock penetrated Jahleel's fogged mind. A dream? He didn't think so. He shook away the cobwebs. He took a breath, and tried to rise from the couch in his living room. No use. Can't do it. He tried again. Nope. He slumped against the pillow. His breath came in rapid gasps now. His heart pounded like a jackhammer. I'm gonna die here.

Knock. Knock.

He closed his eyes, more in exhaustion than prayer. "Oh, Jesus let it be someone to help me. Please, Jesus."

The soft knock again. "Jahleel, you there?"

He knew the voice. Demos. He gathered his strength. "Come in." No use. He couldn't manage more than a whisper.

Rap, rap, rap. Louder this time.

Jahleel tried to catch his breath. "Come. . ." Moments later he heard the latch turn and the door open. His prayer answered.

Demos closed the door and crossed the room. "Don't take this wrong, friend, but you don't look too good. Is your oxygen set at the correct flow?"

"Think so."

He bent over Jahleel, checked the metering device, then took Jahleel's wrist to check his pulse. "Your heart's racing. You need to go to the hospital. I'm going to call an ambulance."

"But. . . but. . ." His breath came in gasps as though he'd run up fifteen flights of stairs.

"No buts. You're going to the hospital." Demos headed for the phone across the room.

"Can't afford. . ."

Demos spun around. "Don't worry about affording anything. I'll find a way to take care of it. Now concentrate on breathing through your nose, not your mouth."

As Demos reached for the phone it rang. He picked it up and spoke, "William's residence." He listened. Brows knit together.

Jahleel turned his head toward Demos. "Who?"

"Just a moment" Demos covered the mouthpiece. "Your doctor's office. They say you missed your appointment this morning."

Jahleel closed his eyes and shook his head.

"My name is Demos, and I'm a friend of Jahleel. I stopped by to check on him a couple of minutes ago. He's not doing well. His heart is racing. He can't catch his breath. I think he needs to go to the hospital. I was about to call an ambulance." He paused and nodded his head. "Yes. Yes. I'll make sure they take him there." Demos hung up the phone, then immediately picked up the receiver and dialed 9-1-1. He asked the system operator to send an ambulance and gave them the address.

Jahleel stared at his friend with wide eyes. He'd never felt fear like this. A word formed on his lips, but no sound came out. His vision narrowed. Darkness closed in. He thought he would faint. So this is what dying is like. Doesn't hurt at all. In the distance he heard Demos.

"The ambulance is coming. They'll take you to UCLA Medical Center."

Jahleel struggled to open his eyes. Demos bent over him. His face and the look he gave were enough. In the man's dark eyes he read compassion, not worry. "Don't. . . don't go."

"I won't leave you, Jahleel." Demos grasped his hand and held it tight. "I'll stay with you in the ambulance. Just be quiet. I'm going to pray until the paramedics come."

Jahleel closed his eyes and felt peace. The hammering of his heart slowed. Demos would be with him. He'd be all right. He remembered how he'd treated this man when they first met. "I'm sorry."

"It's okay. We'll get you to the hospital. Doctor Pang is going to meet us there."

Through a haze, as though it were a dream, he watched Demos answer the door and let the paramedics in the apartment.

The ambulance whizzed across the city, siren wailing. After they parked in one of the ER bays they wheeled Jahleel into the emergency room. One of the paramedics and two nurses transferred him to an ER gurney, and pulled a curtain almost completely around him. Demos sat in an orange plastic chair beside him.

Less than thirty seconds later Doctor Pang's round face peered around the curtain. "Ah. My favorite patient. And this must be your friend."

Demos stood. "I'm glad to meet you. Name's Demos. I won't trouble you with my last name. Too many syllables. Half the people in Athens can't pronounce it."

The doctor laughed, then turned to Jahleel. "Well, well. Took a turn for the worse, I see." He examined the oxygen gauge. "Looks like someone turned up your O-two. Feeling better?"

"Uh-huh."

Doctor Pang's eyes narrowed. Have you been on your oxygen?"

"Uh-huh."

"All the time?"

"Yeah."

"Even at night?"

Didn't the guy believe him? "All the time."

He looked at Jahleel's eyes. Lifted one of the lids. "Hmmm. I'm suspicious your red count is down. That would make things more difficult for your heart." He turned and poked his head outside the curtain. "Nurse. I want a CBC and ABG on Mr. Williams, stat. He looked at Jahleel again. "We're going to run some tests to check your oxygen saturation and blood levels. I'll be back to see you after you've been admitted and are in a room." With a swish around the curtain he was gone.

A slight red-haired girl came to draw a vial of his blood. She made faces as she tried to find a good vein among the scarred tissue in his arms.

After five attempts Jahleel said, "Try here." He pointed to the crook of his wrist.

After the lab tech left with her vials of blood, the nurses poked and prodded on Jahleel some more. Pestered him with questions. Demos helped with the admissions process, and half an hour later Jahleel was in a private room in the coronary care wing. A unit of AB-negative blood flowed, drop by drop, into a vein in Jahleel's left arm.

Doctor Pang came through the doorway. "Good. I see they've started the transfusion. I'll stop by again in a couple hours to see how you're doing."

"When do I . . ."

"You don't, Jahleel. I'm going to keep you here a couple days until I'm sure you'll be fine when I let you go home. You're lucky to have a friend like Demos, here."

Did the doctor mean he'd be dead now, if it weren't for Demos?

"We'll have to check your red count again after this unit of blood. That'll tell us if you need a second unit. Concentrate on resting." He gave a quick smile and left.

A lot of rest he'd get with nurses poking at him, taking his temperature, checking his blood pressure all day and night. Maybe he would've been better off if Demos hadn't come. Better off if he died. He looked at Demos, who seemed to be studying him, almost as if he could read his thoughts.

"You look worried, Jahleel. What's going on in that brain of yours?"

"I was wondering."

"Don't think that."

"How do you know what I'm thinking?"

"Let's say it's a sixth sense. Even back in county lock-up I knew all along what you thought."

"You can't."

"Who says I can't. Now get some rest before the nurse comes to check your blood pressure." Demos chuckled. "And think happy thoughts. I need to go now, but I'll be back." He slipped out of the room and closed the door softly.

Impossible. No one could read his thoughts. But then, Demos always seemed to know. How did he do that?

Chapter 47

Jahleel hated hospitals. The sheets felt like sandpaper. The air smelled like a medicine cabinet, except when the janitors came by, and then the disinfectant overpowered the antiseptic. They'd hooked him up to some infernal machine that beeped every few minutes. He stared at the ceiling and counted the pimples in the texture, much as he'd done when he was in prison. Six days now, and Doctor Pang still refused to let him go home, not that it would do him much good. He couldn't make it to the bathroom without getting winded, and that was with the portable oxygen tank.

The door to his room opened. Demos stepped through. "I don't want to rain on your parade, but you look down."

Jahleel managed a weak smile, then it faded. "Same to ya."

"Good to see your sense of humor isn't gone."

"Yeah, yeah."

"I just talked with your doctor. He told me you're not snapping back like he hoped. He did say something about a clinical trial. He wants to get you in."

"You mean he wants to keep me alive so I can die next year."

"Where's the cynicism coming from?"

Jahleel took in a long breath and let it out. "Caught me. Crack in the mask." He paused to catch his breath. "I don't think there's much use any more." He stopped again to take more deep breaths. "Don't get me wrong. I'm grateful. Hey, man, I wouldn't have any hope of eternal life if you and Pastor Andrew hadn't kept hammering at me." He lay back, exhausted.

"Okay, so you've decided to just quit?"

"Ain't that what's gonna happen? Haul me out of here in a bag? We all go sometime."

"I don't think so, Jahleel." Demos' dark eyes riveted him. "Listen to me now. God wouldn't have led me to your prison cell to have you end like this. You have a gift. You have a way with words. You can write, you can preach. I think God has big plans for you."

Jahleel turned his head away. "I don't know. It just seems so hopeless. I need a new heart instead of this one that's quitting on me." He tapped his chest with a thin index finger. "And I knows I gotta be way down on the transplant list. Now, tell me where's the hope here?"

Demos stepped closer to the hospital bed and leaned over Jahleel. "Look at me. You can't give up. Not now, when it looks like there's no way out. Don't underestimate what God can do. It was hopeless for the children of Israel to leave Egypt, but they did. It was hopeless for them to get across the Red Sea, but they did. It was hopeless for David to go into battle with a slingshot, but he did. It was hopeless for Daniel when they tossed him in the den of lions. It seemed hopeless when the Romans nailed Jesus to the cross. Don't give me this hopeless line. Have you ever thought God is using what you're going through to build your faith?"

Jahleel shook his head. "Not too bad a preacher

yourself."

"I've said my piece. Think about it. I'm going to go now. See you tomorrow." He headed toward the door, then stopped and skewered Jahleel with a piercing look. "I said I'd see you tomorrow."

"I heard you." He paused a beat. "Yeah, Okay, Demos. See ya tomorrow."

"Mean it?"

"Yeah, I mean it. Now go preach to somebody else."

Demos closed the door quietly.

Jahleel turned his attention back to the blemishes on the ceiling. The guy wouldn't leave him alone. What kept Demos working on him like that? Was it worth it to try and keep hoping? I'm just a little pimple on the earth. How in the world can I even think I'm important enough for God to work things out for me. For God to somehow find a new heart for me? He closed his eyes. I don't want to die, God. But my hope's all used up. I need me a Red Sea miracle, and I don't see where it's coming from.

Chapter 48

Tiffany gave her hair a few final strokes with the brush and looked at herself in the mirror. For the most part, her image pleased her. Just the right touch of lip gloss and blush on her cheeks. Eye make-up not too heavy. Something was missing. She wanted to look her best for the meeting that morning with a group of unwed mothers. Her first solo job working for the County Health Department. She would be helping each of the ten women, girls really, navigate their way through the system. Counseling them about the pros and cons of keeping their child, versus giving the infant up for adoption. She wanted to make the right impression, and earn their confidence and trust. She needed something more. Something with a little pizzazz. What should she do? Ah, yes. Carmen's old necklace would set off the pale blue of her eyes. She tiptoed to Carmen's bedroom and slowly twisted the knob. The necklace would do nicely. She didn't want to wake her roommate who'd gone to bed just an hour earlier after working the graveyard shift at the hospital. Ever since they began rooming together, Carmen urged her repeatedly to wear a little more bling. But her past, when she wore too much, held her back.

She spotted the necklace, just costume jewelry really, laying on the dresser. Stepping slowly so she wouldn't wake Carmen Tiffany edged across the room. When she picked the sea blue apatite pendant up, she touched a bottle of nail polish, which clattered as it toppled over and then fell to the floor.

Carmen rubbed the heel of her hand across her eyes. "What. . .? Oh it's you, Tiff."

"Just borrowing your pendant. I didn't mean to wake you. Go back to sleep."

"Oh. You've got that meeting with those girls this morning, don't you?"

"Yeah. Then a seminar this afternoon. Now, go to sleep. I'll see you tonight."

Carmen raised up and looked at Tiffany. "You look great, but what else is new? And the pendant will be just the right touch. Now go and let those girls know they can do anything they set their mind to, just like you did."

Tiffany turned to leave. "I'm expecting Elwina tonight, too. She said she'd stop by. I've written a letter for her to take to Jahleel. I promised her I would, and I must have written it eighteen times. I'm still not sure it's right."

"You don't want to take it to him yourself?"

"I think it's too soon for both of us. I know it is for me."

Carmen lay back in the bed. "Probably so. Go give those girls some hope." A yawn. "I'm going back to sleep. And drive safe."

"I will. Good night." It still sounded weird to Tiffany saying good night at nine-fifteen in the morning. She tiptoed from the room with the pendant.

Ten minutes later her tiny Toyota crawled through the late morning traffic, as she travelled west on Wilshire for the meeting in Westwood. The girls, all pregnant and single, came from varied backgrounds. There were two prostitutes, four college coeds, and the rest high-schoolers or dropouts. She'd been over her talk more than a dozen times. Still, nervous jitters about what she'd say, and how best to say it, troubled her. How much of her own life should she reveal? How much of God's help should she talk about?

A traffic light ahead turned amber. The car in front gunned it through the intersection. She braked to a stop. Engrossed in thought about her talk, and wondering what questions the women would have, she didn't see the light turn green until someone laid on their horn. She pressed the accelerator, intent on getting across so the driver behind her wouldn't be too irritated. She heard the scream of brakes. In her peripheral vision she saw the big SUV hurtling toward her, felt the impact, and heard the grinding of metal against metal. The airbag deployed and smashed into her face. Then nothing.

Chapter 49

Alderon edged between two utility vans on the fourth floor of a parking garage just south of the UCLA Medical Center. He leaned against the side of one van, his legs drawn up and his hands clasped at his knees. With his eyes closed, he looked like an old man taking a nap. A satisfied grin played around his lips.

"You're not sleeping are you?"

Alderon looked up to see Heylel standing between the vehicles. "Of course not, Master. Just waiting for you."

"You have something to report?"

Alderon stood and looked up at Heylel. No matter what form they took, the Master was always taller by four or five inches. "It was beautiful to see. Tiffany was on her way to a meeting, and so distracted that she didn't pay attention to her driving. As luck would have it, an angry driver ran a red light, and rammed into the driver's side of her little car. Sometimes all we need to do is let these humans go about their greedy, selfish ways and they do our work for us. There wasn't anything Paragon could do to help her. I watched as the fire department cut away the door. She looked almost gone when they loaded her in the ambulance. I followed it here. The paramedics were giving her CPR and then inside the ER she flat-lined."

"So Tiffany's dead. Excellent. A shame she stayed in the enemy's camp, but at least she won't be able to witness for them any more."

"Yes, Master. Gone for good. She won't be able to do anything to help the enemy now."

"Paragon's still around? They haven't called him back?"

"Yes. He's so invested in Jahleel, who'll be dead in a few days anyway. Doesn't make sense." Alderon looked out of the parking structure to the hospital where Tiffany took her last breath.

"Don't worry about it. They always fawn over every soul, even when it's hopeless."

Alderon turned to say something, but Heylel had vanished.

Chapter 50

Sunlight brightened the room. Jahleel numbered the days in his journal. This morning would be the tenth day since his surgery. Even the beige hospital walls looked beautiful. Yesterday he walked across the room without being winded. He couldn't believe they'd found a match for his diseased heart in such a short time. He thought his blood type being rare would make the wait longer, perhaps too long; instead he had his Red Sea miracle.

Doctor Pang pushed through the door. "How's my favorite patient feeling today?" He looked at the monitor that recorded Jahleel's blood pressure, pulse, and oxygen utilization. "Sleep well?"

"Feel great, Doc. Never better."

Doctor Pang pulled a stethoscope from his lab coat pocket. "Let me listen to that new heart of yours."

Jahleel pulled the cover down to expose his chest. The cool stethoscope sent an involuntary shiver through his thin frame.

"Good to see your reactions are normal. Hmmm. . ." Doctor Pang always hummed when he began listening, then he'd stop and his brow would furrow as though he heard something troubling. No frown today. "Pumping on all cylinders."

"That's good to hear."

"I've been over your lab work from last night. You seem to be tolerating the drugs to suppress rejection, and they're doing their job. No signs of anything amiss. Looks like we found the perfect heart for you. Of course we might have to alter the dosage a bit, but that's routine. Just means we'll have to check it out every week or so for a while."

A wide smile lit Jahleel's face. "Good to know. Now I can finish school. By the way, Doc, when are you going to let me have visitors?"

"A day or two. What was it you're studying again?"

"I'm going back to Bible college. After I gave my life to God, he called me to be a preacher."

"Ah, yes, I remember. Good for you." Doctor Pang's eyes brightened. "I do what I can for the body, you're going to help people with their souls. A noble profession."

A momentary silence fell between them. Jahleel didn't quite know how to respond. "I just hope I'm able to go wherever God sends me."

"I'm sure you will be. You've got a good strong heart now to take you there. I'll see you again on my evening rounds." Doctor Pang gave a final smile, turned, and left the room.

Jahleel picked up his journal from the bedside stand. Time to review yesterday's notes, then add some thoughts for this morning. He wanted to begin writing more than little vignettes about his experience. He wanted to tell his story to anyone who would listen. He pushed the button to call the nurse, then opened the book to the last page he'd written.

He heard the door open. The nurse never came that fast. He glanced up. Not the nurse, but his old cell-mate Demos walked in.

"You up for a visitor?"

"What's the matter, man? You look like you lost your best friend."

Demos focused on the floor for a moment, then back at Jahleel. A half smile flitted across his face. "Someone I cared about died a few days ago. A friend asked me to watch out for her. Keep her safe. I couldn't."

"I'm sorry."

"Me too, but God always seems to be able to turn the bad into good. So. . . You're looking fit. Writing in your journal?"

"Yeah. Yesterday I wrote about you hounding me when we was cell-mates." He made a face. "Sorry about the bad grammar. Still trying not to sound like I got no education." Jahleel couldn't help but smile. "I'm glad you kept after me, man. And I'm glad you encouraged me. . . No, preached to me about not giving up. Tell me, how did you get in here? All I see are nurses and doctors."

Demos chuckled. "Snuck by the nurse's station."

"If they catch you, they'll chase you out. Doc says a couple days 'til they let me have visitors. Something about not wanting to expose me to too many germs."

"Don't worry. . . nobody'll find me here."

"I just rang for the nurse to raise my bed so I can write in my journal."

"I think they're busy with something else. Besides I won't stay long." Demos pushed the control buttons to raise the head of the bed. "How's that?"

"Perfect. Thanks."

"The reason I came was to bring you this letter. And to tell you a secret." He held out a lavender envelope.

As soon as he saw it Jahleel knew who wrote the letter. He remembered the one she'd sent while he was in prison. What would this one say? His finger trembled as he tore open the envelope. The same flowing script so soft and gentle like she'd been when he first met her. Before he'd turned her on to drugs. Before he'd used her.

Dear Jahleel,
   I heard you've given your life to the Lord.
I'm glad, and hope you're discovering
how liberating and full life can be on His side.
   The other day a friend told me your heart
isn't responding to the medication and you've
had to quit Bible College. I'm sorry for that.
I know if you could preach the message of Jesus
with the fervor you preached a hedonistic life,
you'd be able to lead so many to Christ.
   The real reason I'm writing is to let you
know I forgave you long ago for taking me
down the road to drugs and prostitution.
I pray every day for God to find a way to
heal your heart. You'll make a great
ambassador for the Lord, just like the apostle
Paul did. Don't give up, Jahleel.
                    In Christian love,
                    Tiff.

Jahleel laid the letter on his lap and wiped at his eyes with a corner of the sheet. He looked at Demos. "How did you get this letter?"

"One of the Lord's small miracles."

"Not going to tell me are you?"

Demos shook his head.

"She's praying for me, Demos. She said. . ." He picked up the letter and scanned the page. "She said, 'I

221

pray every day for God to find a way to heal your heart'. I don't deserve that, Demos. What I did to that girl." He closed his eyes and shook his head. "And she's forgiven me. I wish I could take back all the hurt I caused her, but I know the only thing I can do is be thankful. Maybe when they let me out of here. . ."

"I'm sure, like God forgives us before we ask. . . we only need to accept it. . . It's good to know Tiffany has already forgiven you."

"You mentioned you had a secret to tell me too."

Silence ensued.

"What, man? Tell me."

"I'm not who you think I am, Jahleel."

"Who. . . who are you?"

"You know where it says in the Bible God isn't willing that any should perish?"

"Yeah."

"That's one of the reasons I'm here. It's why I got tossed in your cell at county lock-up. You've known me since then as Demos, but I also lived in your apartment building."

"Huh? I don't remember you."

"Up on the third floor. You remember Elwin Hunter?"

"What?" Jahleel's brows knit together. "How? Hunter was a tall skinny white dude. You're short and dark."

"Yes. There's nothing the matter with your memory. I've been a lot of other people, too. My real name is a heavenly one. It's Paragon."

"Huh? Who. . . what? You trying to tell me you're from heaven? That'd make you. . . "

Demos smiled and nodded. "Yeah, an angel. Oh, one more thing. Your new heart. Ten days ago it beat in Tiffany's chest. It seems you and she had the same blood type. All the other antigens, and things they test, they all matched."

Jahleel stared at Demos, mouth open, brain not registering the information.

"She's. . . ?"

"She's gone Jahleel. A car accident. She'd signed a donor pledge when she got her license to drive. Her lungs, her kidneys, and liver have gone to others. Some blind person sees because of her corneas. You, my friend, have her heart."

"What?" He held up the letter in a shaking hand as tears ran down his cheeks. "She. . . How?"

Demos began to glow with an ethereal aura like a light bulb slowly being filled with energy. "My work's done. You are charged with telling this story, Jahleel. Some won't believe you. Others will. You are to be Christ's ambassador to your generation. Preach to the desolate and the despised, to the poor and the rich, just as Paul preached to the Gentiles. God's love will flow through you to them. I must go now. Farewell my friend."

With a blinding flash Demos vanished.

Made in the USA
Charleston, SC
08 May 2016